Painting *Seascapes* In Watercolor

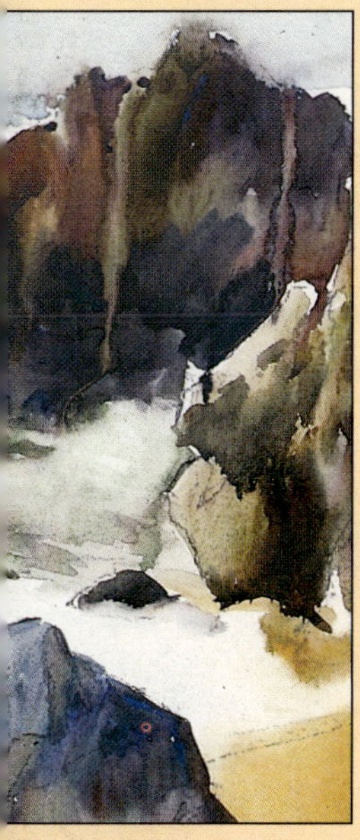

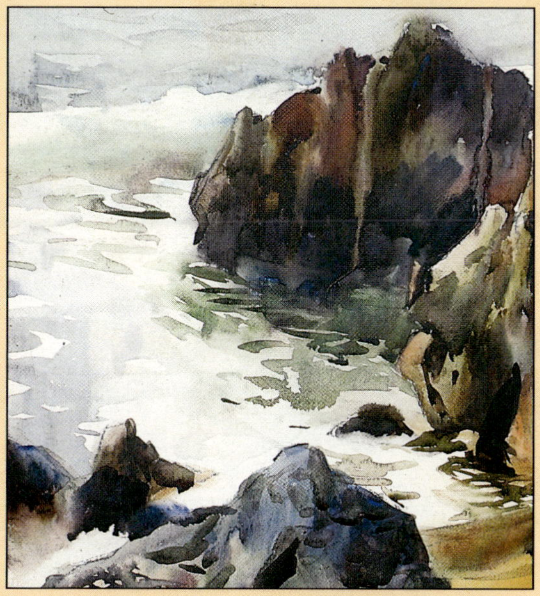

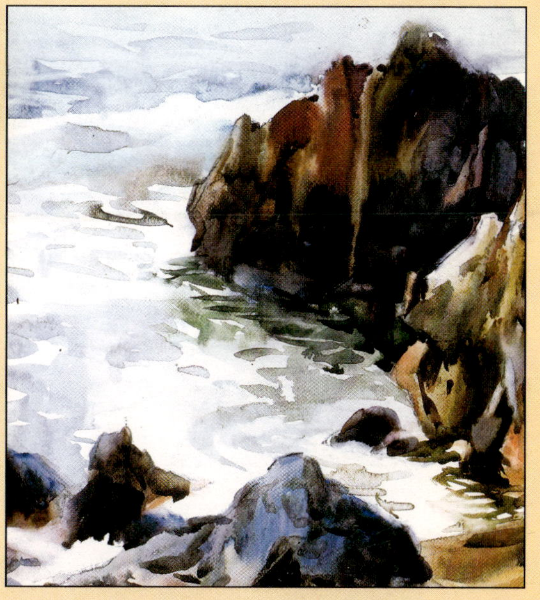

The Watson-Guptill Painting Library is a collection of books that teaches you the art of drawing and painting by showing you what professional artists do and how they do it. Each book in the series concentrates on one technique or procedure (oil, watercolor, acrylics, pastels, colored pencils, and so on) and one particular theme (landscape, seascape, still life, figure, portrait, and so on). The introduction to each book consists of teachings that relate to the specific theme and subject matter. This book is concerned with *painting seascapes in watercolor*, and the introduction deals, through examples, with composition, value, and color.

What is truly remarkable about this series is that each book teaches you about subject matter; choosing a subject, composition, interpretation, color harmonization; the effects of light, shade, and value; cool, warm, and broken color ranges; and much more. These books are designed to impart all the techniques, secrets, and tricks of the trade. The experience and skill of various professional artists is shared with you and illustrated line by line, stroke by stroke, step by step, with the aid of dozens of photographs taken while each artist paints his or her picture.

I personally directed the teamwork that went into all these books, and am most proud of the results. I can honestly state that *I truly believe that this series of books can really teach you how to paint.*

José M. Parramón
Watson-Guptill Painting Library

Introduction to the theme

1

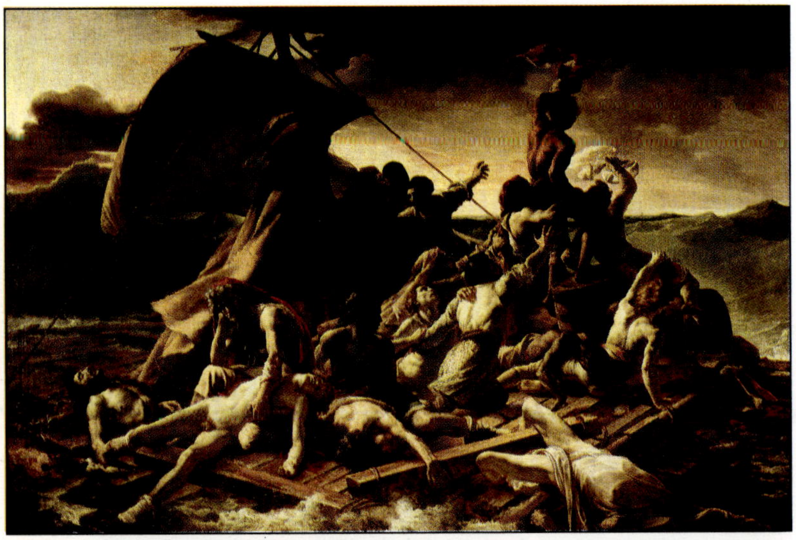

2

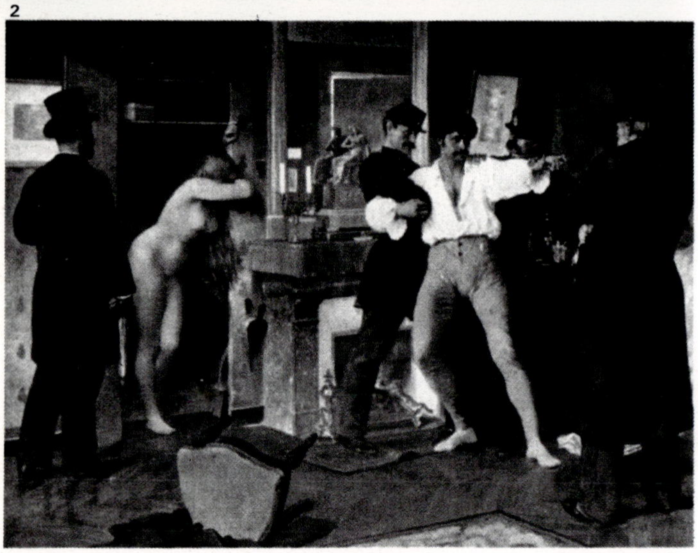

Fig. 1. Théodore Géricault, *The Raft of the Medusa*, Louvre, Paris. This painting is a fine example of the monumental, historic painting genre.

Fig. 2. Jules Garnier, *The Proof of Adultery*, Louvre, Paris. In this monumental, heroic painting, the scene becomes overtheatrical. It represents a vision far from the world of reality.

On July 4, 1816, the French frigate the *Medusa*, manned by a crew of four hundred, ran aground near Cape d'Arguin on the Mauritanian coast.

The deserted and wild nature of the area where they had been forced to land was such that the captain of the vessel ordered a raft, capable of holding 150 of his men, to be built. This was to be sent out, charged with finding a port and requesting help. The raft was towed by a lifeboat, and even though those on board the two vessels had sworn not to separate, after sailing two miles the crew of the lifeboat cut the tow rope, leaving the raft and those aboard to drift helplessly for thirteen days and nights. During these thirteen days, conditions on board the raft of the *Medusa* were an inferno.

Many of the sailors got drunk, mutinied, and were shot. There was hand-to-hand fighting with axes and knives, murders, and some of the crew even ate the meat of their dead companions. On July 17, the brig *Argos* rescued the remaining fifteen survivors on the raft.

The tragedy of the *Medusa* moved French public opinion to the extent that the incident became the prime subject matter of journalists, poets, illustrators, and painters. The celebrated romanticist artist Théodore Géricault chose this subject for one of the largest pictures ever painted in the history of art, *The Raft of the Medusa*. The painting, measuring 197″×276″ (5×7 m), is reproduced in figure 1 on this page.

When preparing to paint this enormous picture, Théodore Géricault interviewed several of the survivors and consulted the reports published at the time. He also visited the morgue and studied the different states of decomposition of the bodies, and went to the lunatic asylum to sketch some of the members of the crew who had gone mad as a result of the tragedy. At Le Havre, he observed the movement of the waves, and he even constructed a model of the raft in his studio. Géricault did all this to dramatize the sense of reality of his picture.

The monumental, heroic paintings

This treatment of the subject matter of a painting was typical of the academic painters of the 19th century. Their vision of composition was a theatrical scene in which the bodies and objects were similar to actors positioned by a stage manager—with light illuminating each object individually and in which color was merely an additional element to identify the objects.

Thus, we come to the era of the monumental, heroic paintings. These enormous canvases almost always depict historical, mythological, literary, or religious themes. Many of these paintings filled the Official Galleries of Paris.

Impression, Sunrise

On April 15, 1874, there was an exhibition of 160 works by the 30 artists of the Artist's Company of Painters, Sculptors, and Engravers in the gallery of the photographer Nadar, in Paris. This was the first exhibition, held without the blessing of the Official Gallery, of the work of a group of painters whose style later came to be known as *Impressionism*.

The Impressionists owe the coining of this term to the art critic Louis Leroy. He wrote a derisive, ironic review centered on Claude Monet's picture, *Impression, Sunrise* (fig. 3).

But the society of the time, locked in this bourgeois way of life, could not accept revolution or change of any kind, even in the field of art. The Impressionists became the object of ferocious attacks—one of the most notable was by the art critic Albert Wolff in the Parisian newspaper, *Le Figaro*, about the second Impressionist exhibition of 1876.

The leaders of the Impressionist movement included, besides the battling Monet, such painters as Jean-Frédéric Bazille, Alfred Sisley, Pierre-Auguste Renoir, Camille Pissarro, Paul Cézanne, Edgar Degas, and Berthe Morisot. Another woman artist, the American Mary Cassatt, met Degas a few years after the first exhibition and was invited to show her work with the rest of the group.

April 1876. Second Impressionist exhibition. Review by Albert Wolff in the newspaper *Le Figaro*.

"Five or six alienated artists, among them a woman, a group of unfortunates inflicted with the madness of ambition, have come together in order to exhibit their work. Some people find this type of thing hilarious, but my own heart is heavy. These so-called artists refer to themselves as intransigent, as revolutionaries. They take a canvas, paint and paintbrushes, throw on a few tones at random and plunge recklessly to work. It is the same as with the inmates of the Ville-Evrard lunatic asylum, who pick up stones from the paths and call them diamonds. Oh, sorry spectacle of human vanity taken to the limits of madness! Please, try to make Mister Pissarro understand that trees are not violet, that the sky is not the color of fresh butter, that what he paints cannot be seen anywhere on earth and that no person in his right mind could swallow such aberrations.... Please, try to make Mister Degas see reason. Tell him that there are such qualities in art as drawing, color and execution. He will laugh in your face and accuse you of being reactionary. Try to explain to Mister Renoir that the torso of a woman is not a lump of decomposing flesh with green-violet stains, like a putrifying corpse.... There is also a woman in the group, as there is in all the most famous gangs. Her name is Berthe Morisot, and she is quite a sight to behold. In this woman, the feminine graces are reduced to the level of the unbridled passions of a delirious spirit."

3

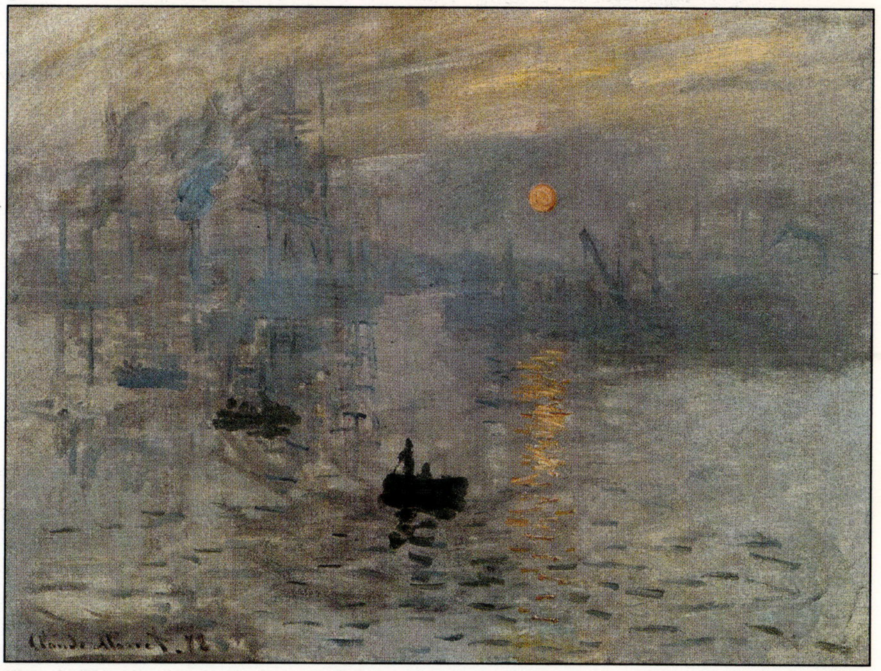

Fig. 3. The painting *Impression, Sunrise*, by Claude Monet (Marmottan Museum, Paris), was the detonator for the first revolution in modern art.

The Impressionist revolution

Figs. 4 to 6. Shown here are some of the motives that served as the inspiration for some of the Impressionist painters. Claude Monet, *Peacocks*, Orsay Museum, Paris (fig. 4); Claude Monet, *Europe Bridge, Saint-Lazare Station*, Marmottan Museum, Paris (fig. 5); and Edgar Degas, *Woman Stepping into the Bath*, The Art Institute of Chicago (fig. 6).

"What should make up the contents of a picture? What subjects or motives should a picture be inspired by?" It is not difficult to imagine this group of "young revolutionaries," in the words of the writer Émile Zola. They would meet in one of the famous cafés of the time, La Brasserie des Martyrs or the Café Guerbois, and try to find answers to those questions while criticizing and pouring scorn on the pictures being shown in the Salon that year.

4

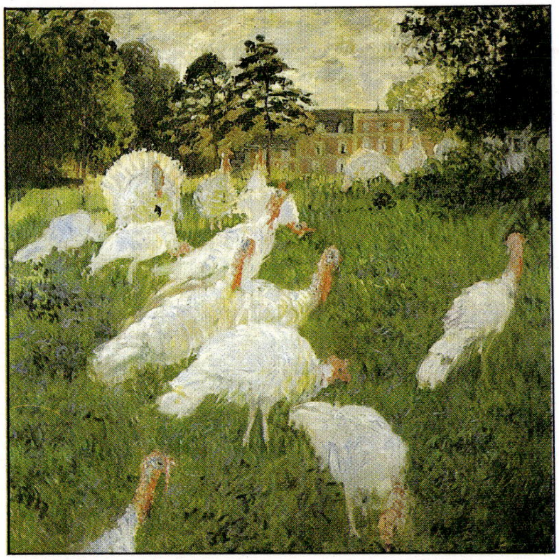

The reply was clear and emphatic. The painter, without preconceived ideas or preparation, should capture life itself, as it is, real and natural.

This is why they decided to paint *motives*, which are quickly made impressions of everyday occurrences that at first glance might seem trivial.

The seemingly trivial as the themes chosen by Monet were such as the meanderings of a group of peacocks (fig. 4) or the smoky roar of railway engines coming into the station (fig. 5). Degas painted the intimate moments of women in their daily routines, an example of which can be seen in figure 6.

What constituted the greatest affront to the conventions of the time—more than Pleinairism, the emphasis on painting subjects out-of-doors, or the use of a palette of light colors—was the brazen exhibition of paintings that were, to the critics of the age, merely quick, spontaneous sketches. These paintings depicted commonplace motives which dared to disdain the grand themes of art.

5

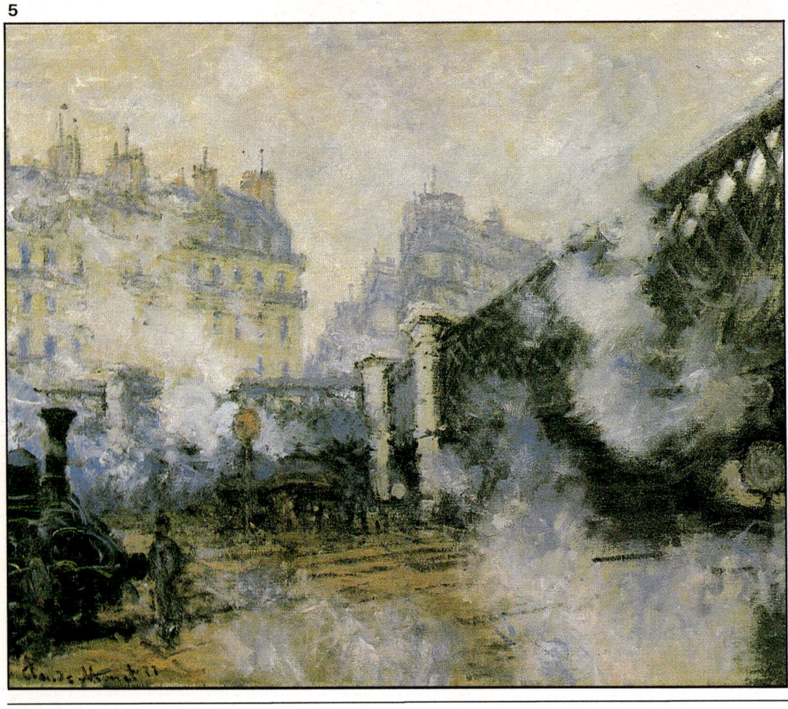

6

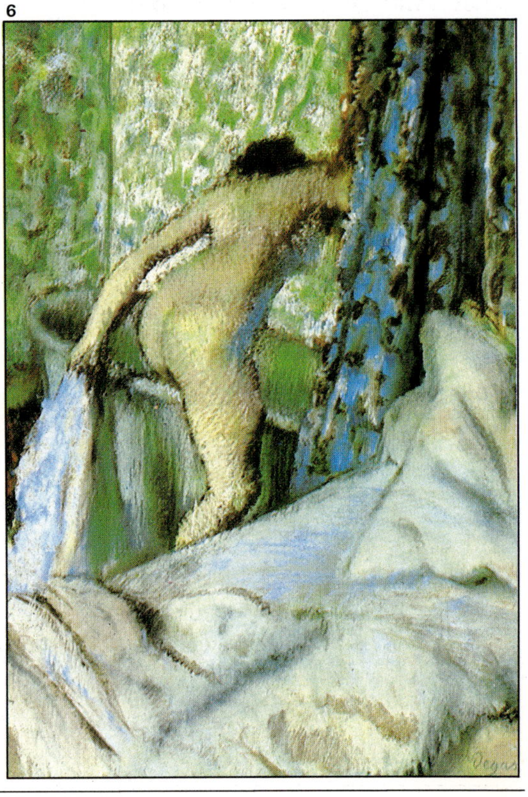

The themes of the Impressionists

What we now think of as the great contribution of Impressionism to the history of art—the introduction of new motives, the representation of atmosphere, the use of pure colors, the originality of framing, and so on—were not achieved overnight. Following the dictates of Pleinairism, some of these young painters descended on the beaches of northern France to portray the impressions they perceived from that landscape. At Saint-Adress, Le Havre, or Dieppe, the Impressionist painters, too, studied the movement of the waves, but with what different intentions to those of Géricault! The Impressionists demonstrated that the features and salient points of a landscape could fire their imagination and inspire them. In other words, a landscape could stand on its own as the central motive of a painting.

Monet, Bazille, Sisley, and the veteran Johan Jongking and Eugène Boudin discovered the continuously changing effects of light. They saw that local color and the color of shadows were made up of more than one color. And, inspired by the theories of color harmony of Eugène Cheverul, they put all their efforts into recording the changes of light when reflected on a continuously moving surface, such as that of water, as you can see in figures 7 and 8.

In painting a variety of themes, the Impressionists followed a number of revolutionary new concepts, most of which are still valid to this day.

Finally, Impressionism triumphed, when artists such as Paul Signac, Georges Seurat, Vincent van Gogh, Paul Gauguin, Henri Matisse, and André Derain introduced a more radical, revolutionary style—known as Postimpressionism or *fauvism* (wild beasts), which stayed true to the subject matter and the achievements of Impressionism. Camille Manclair described this new style as "a pot of paint thrown into the eyes of the observer."

7

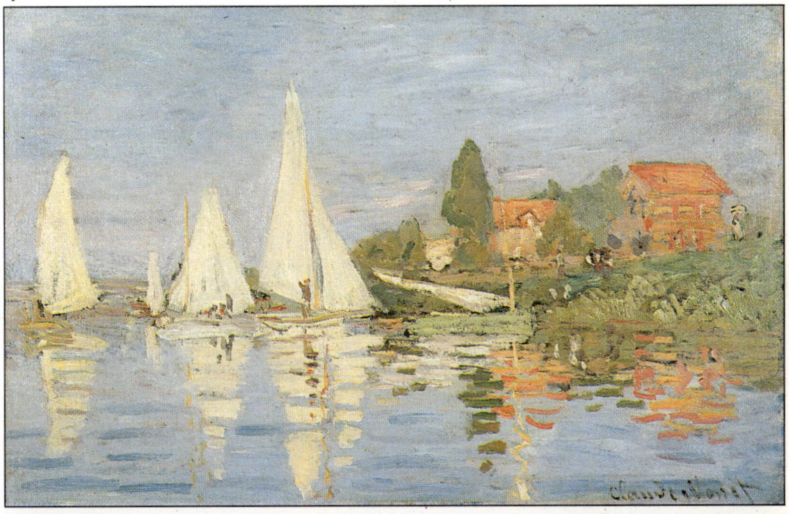

8

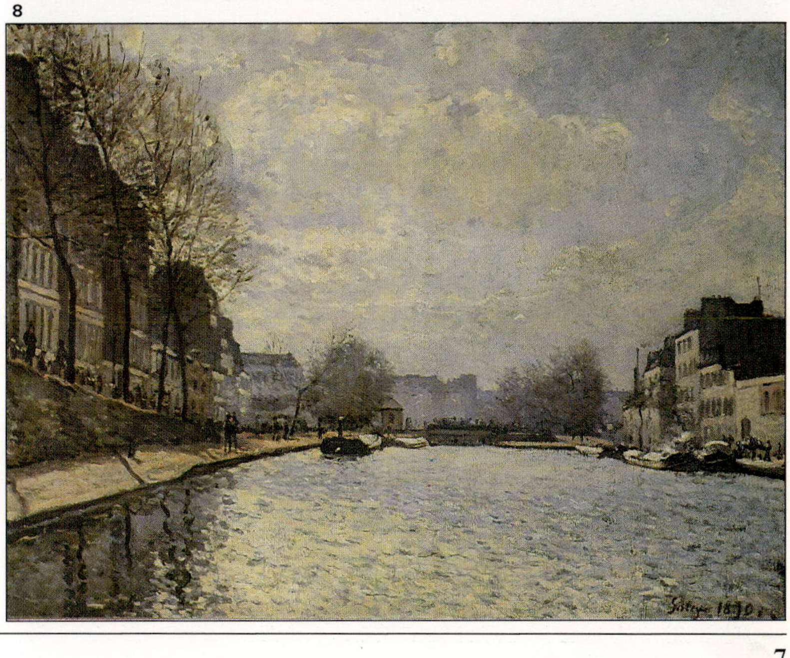

Figs. 7 and 8. Claude Monet, *Boat Race at Argenteuil*, Orsay, Museum, Paris (fig. 7); Alfred Sisley, *San Martin Canal*, Louvre, Paris (fig. 8). The effects of the light on water fired the imagination of the Impressionist painters, who went out into the open air to paint landscapes and seascapes.

Choosing a subject

Fig. 9. Well, we have walked around the port for a while, looking for a suitable subject. We have found a subject that seems to offer possibilities. However, we do not rush into things. To make the most of a subject, you should study it before starting to paint, and a good way of doing this is by framing the picture.

The great lesson that the Impressionists passed on to posterity was the demystification of subject matter. They taught us to think of any object, any moment, as worthy of being painted.

However, their apparent nonchalance or random selection of subject was not, in reality, so great. "To judge what themes are suitable for painting, and what are not, requires great discernment," stated the English painter Sir Joshua Reynolds. The Impressionist painters knew and understood themes really well.

They knew that three factors are of outstanding importance in the choice of subject:

knowing how to observe, which means the ability to identify and select the most appropiate framing, lighting, and point of view for a subject;
composition, or the study of the formal and chromatic structure of a subject; and *interpretation*, the adjustments and modifications that are made to bring the subject closer to the "inner vision" of the artist.

9

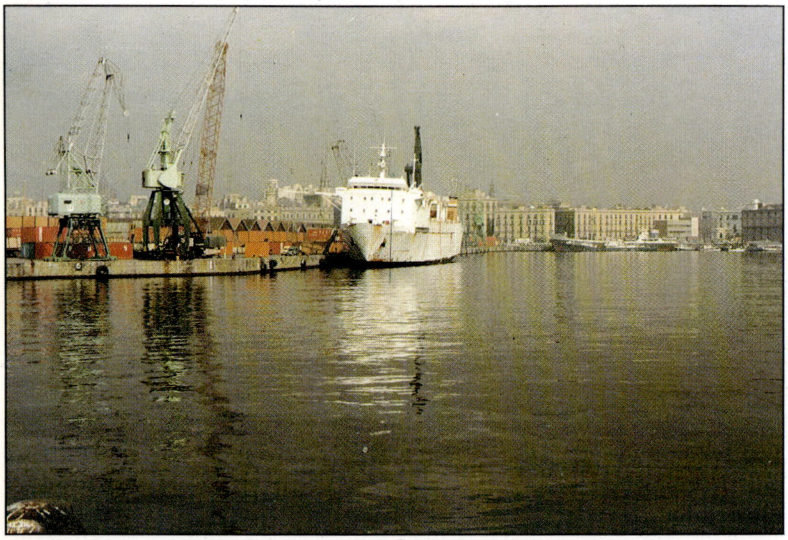

10

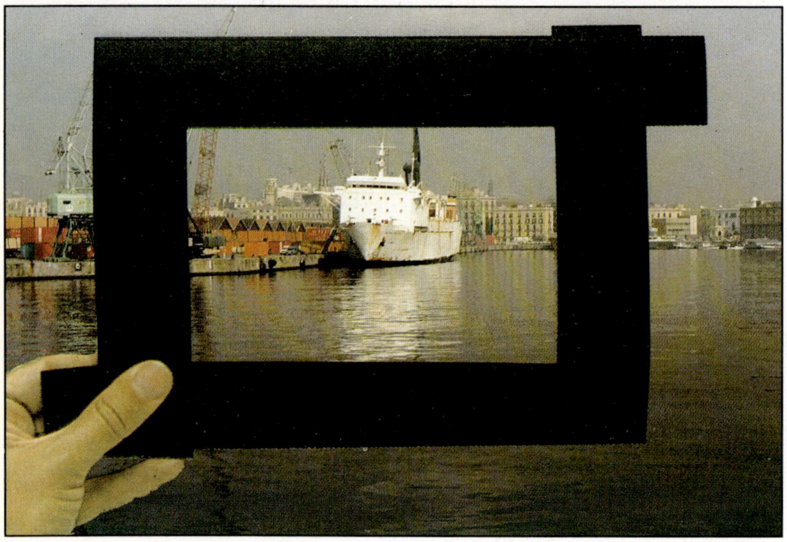

Framing

Framing enables you to determine the part or space of the subject you want to paint. A frame helps you to calculate the size of the objects in a picture according to their position as well as to the proximity of the frame. This frame is simple to construct, if desired, by using just two right-angled pieces of black cardboard, or by shaping your hands into the same shape as a picture frame.

You should always focus the frame on the center of interest of the subject, as this will be the characterizing feature of your painting. This simple rule allows you to evaluate the different possibilities of a picture and to discard those that make the center of interest smaller or less forceful.

Fig. 10. With the aid of this simple device, we try out different possibilities until we find the right framing, one that makes the ship the central focus, but not too forceful. We also want to avoid a wide background, which would take away the focus from the ship.

Point of view

The point of view refers to the different angles or heights from which you observe the subject matter—from one side, from above, from below, and so on (fig. 11).

Once you have observed the subject you have to find the most effective angle. The point of view should bring out the forms and the color contrasts that enrich the composition, emphasizing the subject according to your intentions.

Lighting

When selecting a subject that you plan to paint outdoors, it is of the utmost importance to consider the direction, intensity, and quality of the natural light.

Unless you have decided to paint on a cloudy day, it is advisable to work before or after midday. At noon, the sunlight will fall perpendiculary onto the objects of the picture so that they will have hardly any shadow. It is also important to make sure that the sun does not shine directly onto the canvas. In such a case, you could be dazzled by the light, which may make you darken your color range (fig. 12).

11

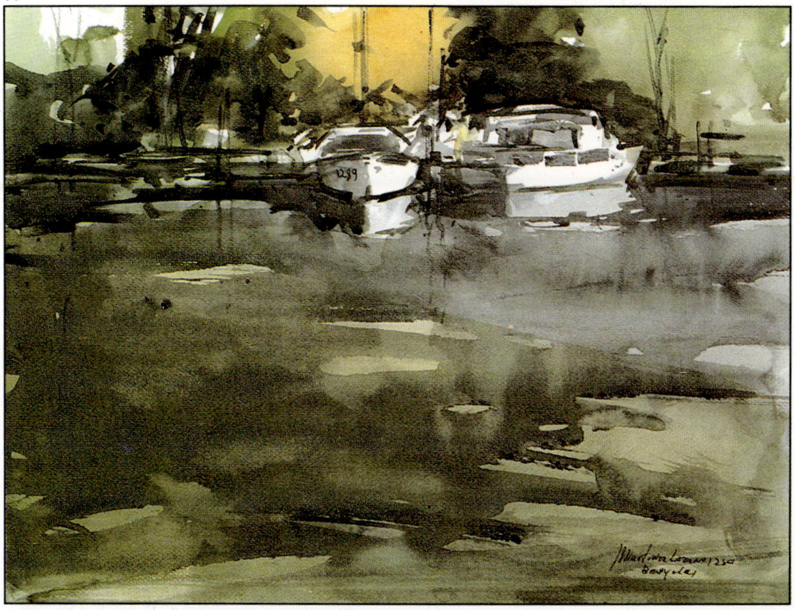

12

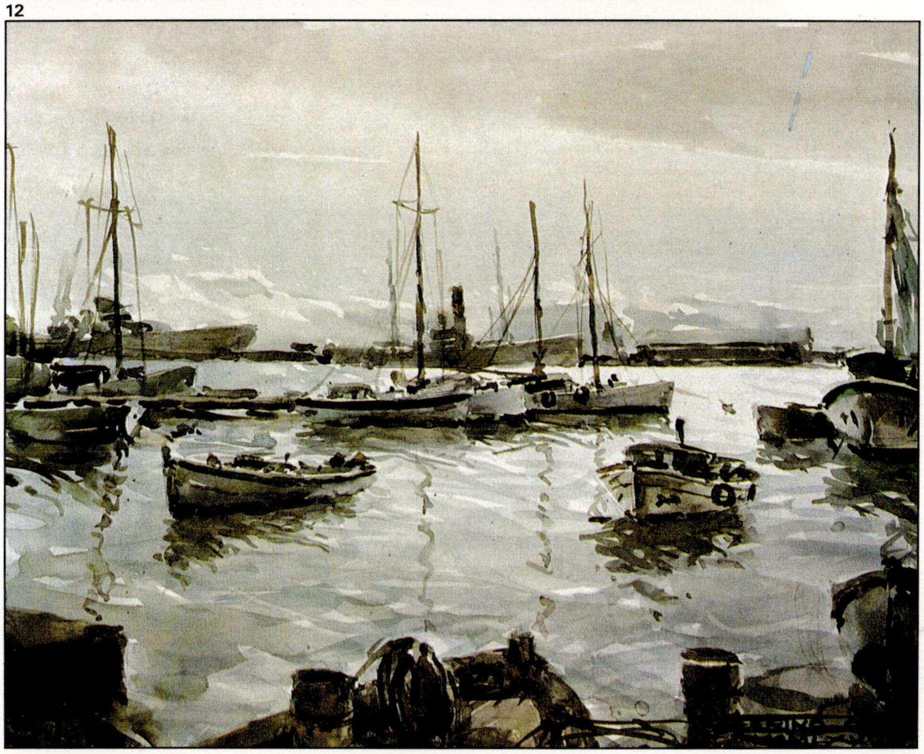

Fig. 11. In this painting, Martínez Lozano has taken a low point of view. By placing the horizon line in the upper half of the picture, he creates a greater sense of space. It draws your attention away from the foreground, occupied by the sea, toward the background, where the only figurative elements of the painting, the boats, are to be found.

Fig. 12. The soft, dim, and somewhat melancholy light of a cloudy day can be ideal for painting particular themes. In the work shown here, *Lumínicas*, Ceferino Olivé creates an evocative atmosphere, totally suited to both the theme and the technique, a seascape in watercolor.

Composing a painting

13

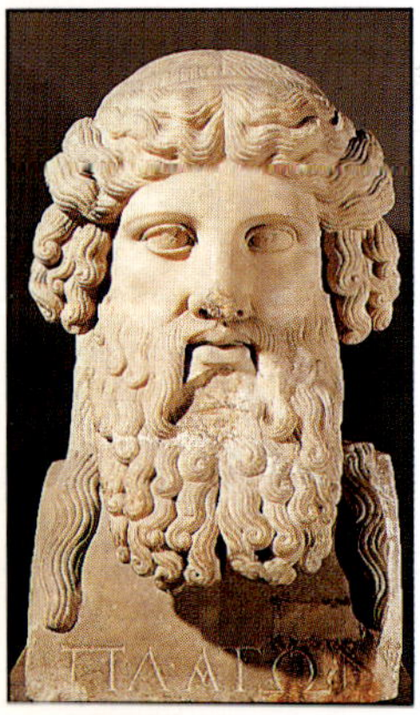

Fig. 13. Plato, one of the most famous philosophers of antiquity, contributed his own concept on the controversial theme of composition. He stated that the solution lay in the correct balance of two principles, unity and variety, which, though apparently opposites, can complement one another.

Composition

What is composition? According to the Penguin *Dictionary of Art and Artists*, it is "the art of combining the elements of a picture into a satisfactory visual whole."

But, what is the meaning of "satisfactory?" The Greek philosopher Plato (fig. 13) gives us a clue when he affirms that "To compose is to find unity in variety."

This is no riddle. It means that when dealing with any subject, you must look for the variety of form, color, and line that attracted your attention and will catch the attention of the viewer.

But it also means that this variety must correspond to an overall unity. There must not be so much variety as to distract or disperse interest from the central focus of the subject.

There are, then, several factors that you must bear in mind when you go out to paint a subject—looking for an interesting and attractive composition for your picture. First, you have to remember that there is an artistically perfect proportion for each and every space. This proportion was defined by the Roman architect Vitruvius in his law of the "golden section", where a line is divided so that the smaller dimension is to the greater as the greater is to the whole.

There are also various practical hints that can help you to study and try out the different possibilites offered by any particular subject. One of these is the use of compositional plans.

Compositional plans

If we accept the premise that the shapes that attract our attention the most, which we find the easiest to observe and recall, are geometric forms, then we will not be surprised to learn that artists have always used these forms when making compositional plans. Among the oldest of these are the pyramid-shaped or triangular symmetrical plan, which was already in use during the Renaissance, and Rembrandt's diagonal, a non symmetrical plan. These and other plans—L-, Z-, C-, or O-shaped, for example—are helpful devices in composing a picture. When trying to find the ideal composition, it is helpful to squint your eyes to eliminate small details. This will enable you to concentrate on the masses and colors of your composition.

14

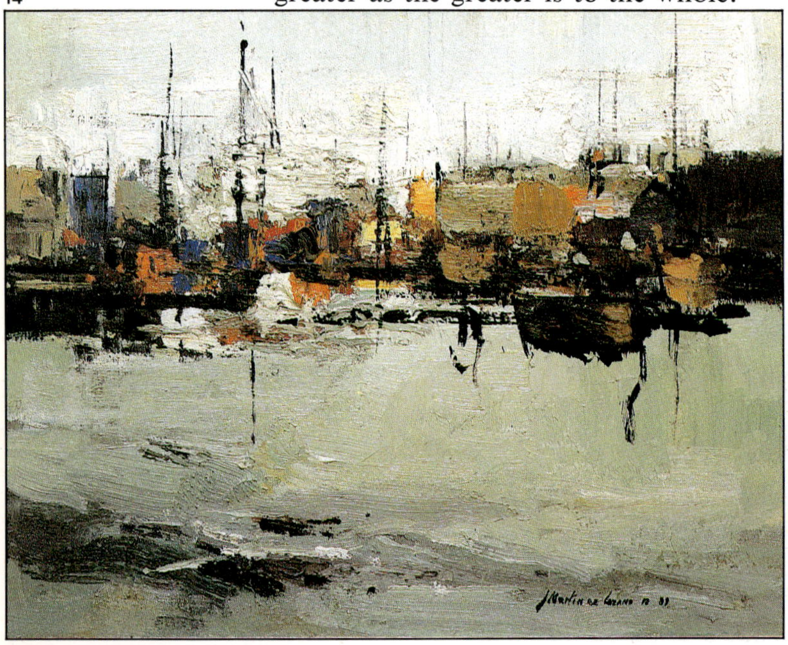

15

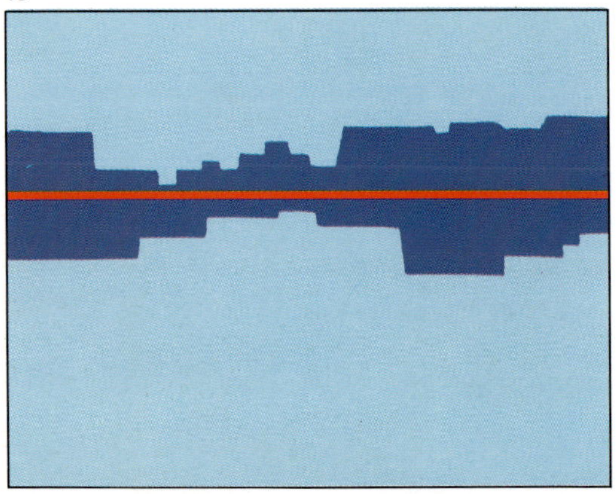

Figs. 14 and 15. Martínez Lozano, *Cantabrian Port*. In this work, the artist has used the "Golden section" as his base for the spatial distribution of his elements. The diagram (fig. 15) shows the mathematical proportions of the painting. You can see that the horizon line coincides with the red line in figure 15, which defines the ideal part of the picture for the center of focus to be placed.

Sketches and preliminary studies

An artist with years of experience can often decide right away if a particular subject is suitable for painting. But it is always a good idea to do a quick sketch or two of a first impression, using a pencil, watercolors, wax crayons, colored pencils, and so on. Besides confirming the framing of the picture and the effects of light and shade, you can also perfect the subject. For instance, you can reinforce a color tendency in the foreground, do a close-up of the center of focus, or even remove specific elements from your picture. It is at this moment that you can make the subject your own. Nowadays, these sketches and preliminary studies can be complemented by the use of another medium—photography.

16

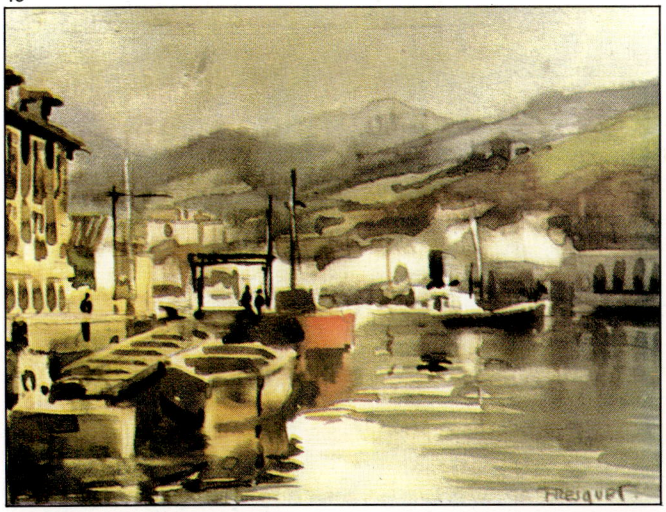

17

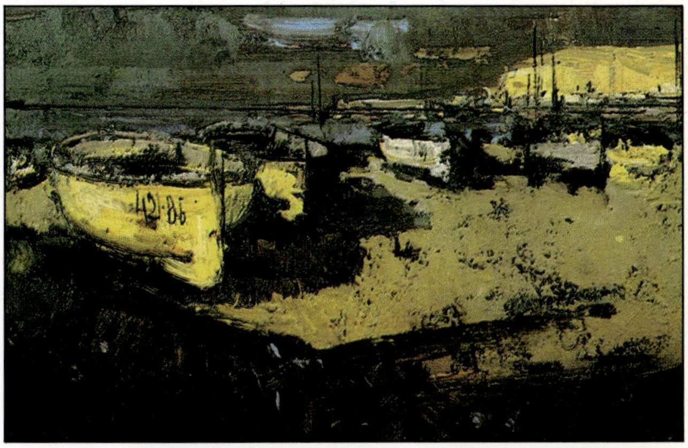

19

20

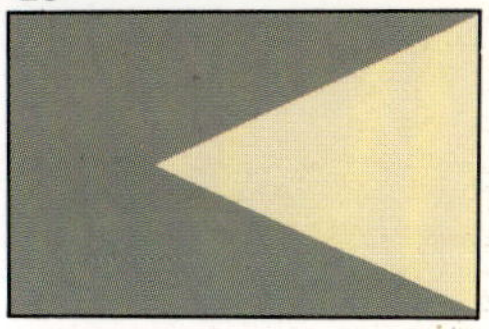

18

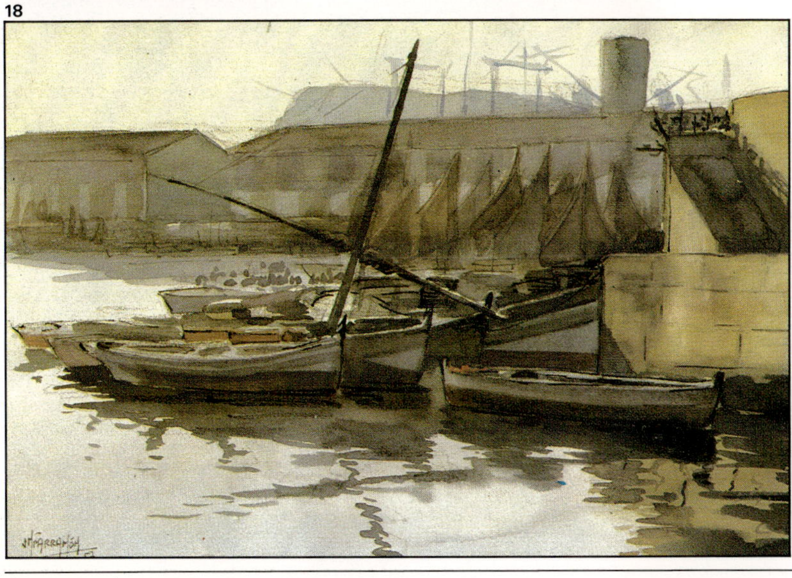

21

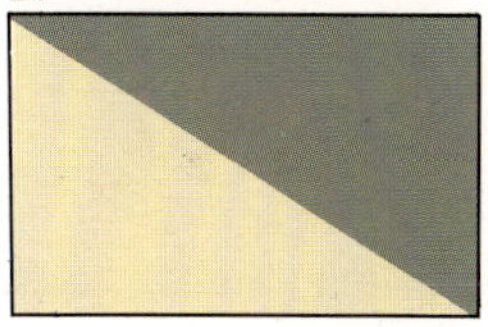

Figs. 16 to 21. Reproduced here are some examples of the work of Guillem Fresquet (fig. 16), Martínez Lozano (fig. 17), and J. M. Parramón (fig. 18). The geometrical compositional plans are obvious. From the most traditional, in the shape of an inverted L or a diagonal line (figs. 19 and 21) in the paintings by Fresquet and Parramón, to the most daring wedge-shaped plan by Martínez Lozano (fig. 20).

Photography, a valuable ally

The influence of photography on the Impressionist painters is universally recognized. Gustave Courbet (1819-1877), for example, used photographs of nude models when painting his pictures of bathers. The equestrian paintings by Degas give the impression of rapid movement captured by the lens of a camera.

The *camera obscura*, forerunner of the photographic camera, was used by numerous artists such as Leonardo da Vinci, Francesco Guardi, and Antonio Canaletto. It is true to say that artists have generally made use of the technical innovations of their times.

Photography allows you to capture different visions of the same subject, varying the point of view and the framing so that you can select the best one for your painting back in the studio. Remember, though, that a photograph should be interpreted, not copied. The role of the photograph for the artist is to round off a session in the open air—recording and preserving that instant, that first impression.

22

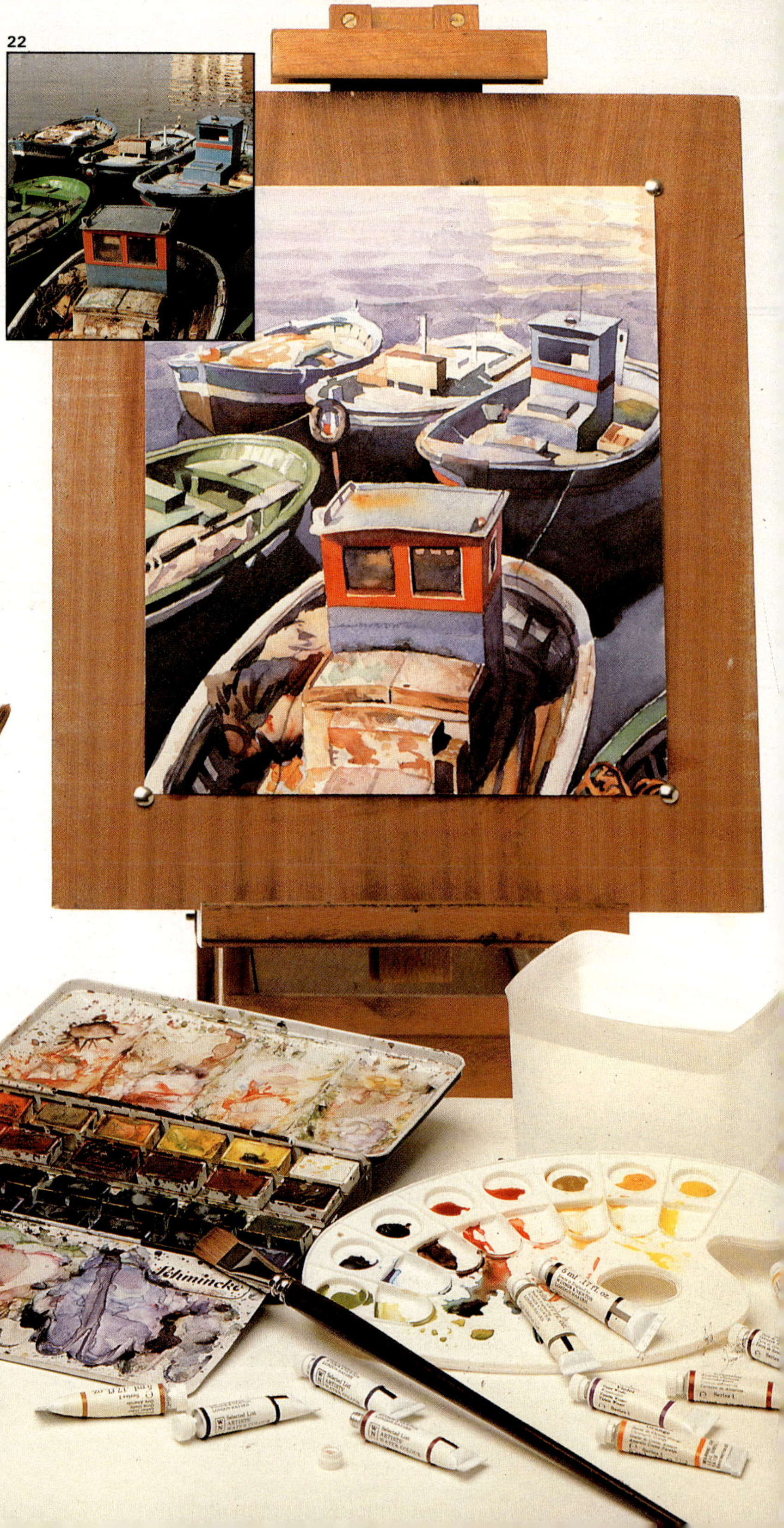

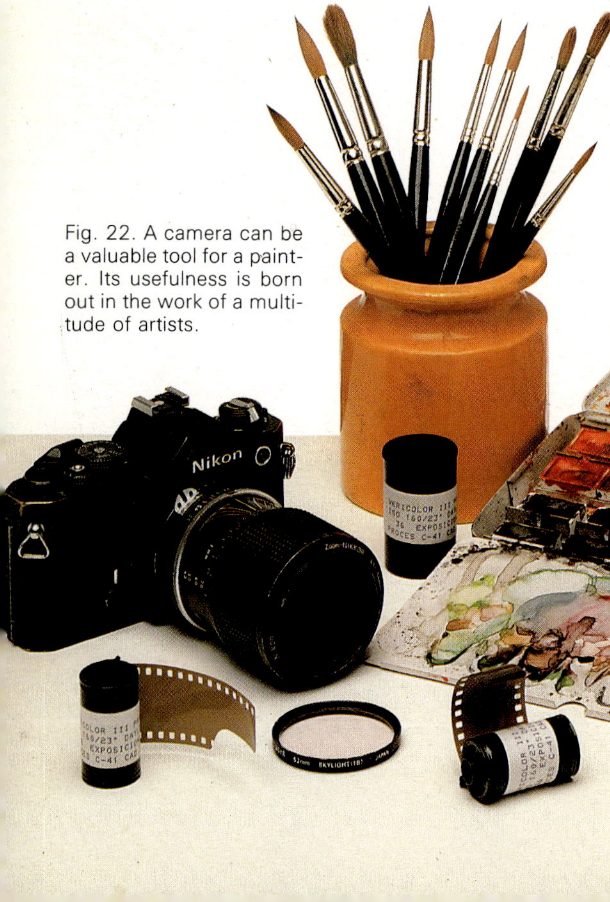

Fig. 22. A camera can be a valuable tool for a painter. Its usefulness is born out in the work of a multitude of artists.

Interpretation

The illustrations on this page provide a practical example of how to use a camera as an auxiliary medium in the selection and interpretation of a subject.

The spot chosen for the painting was a corner of a seaport where fishing boats moored. Four days before starting the picture, I went to the port, and, observing the scene from all directions, I made several sketches and took a number of photos. I finally chose the one at the bottom of the page (fig. 27).

In thc studio, I drcw a plan for my picture, with a different interpretation from the image I had captured in the photo. I changed the perspective and point of view, added a fragment of the port and the moorings in the foreground, and altered the cool color range into a broken color range with a warm tendency.

The result of this interpretation can be seen in the painting I then made (fig. 28).

23
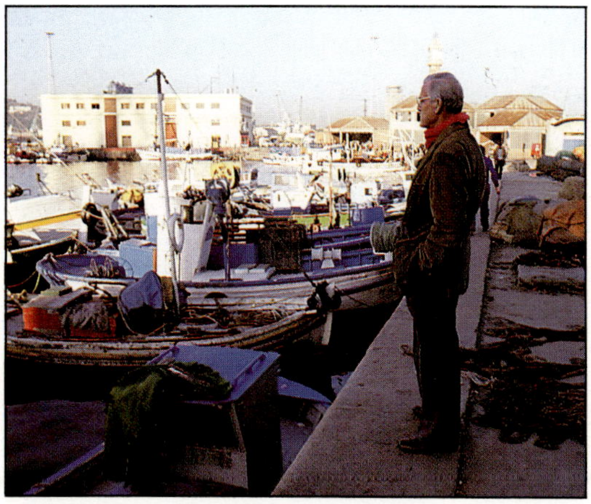

Figs. 23 to 28. Going out to ''paint with the camera.'' This valuable auxiliary medium captures and retains pictures of the various possibilities that can later be transformed into paintings (figs. 24 to 26). Back in the studio, the photo of the chosen subject (fig. 27) is of great assistance to the artist in painting the definitive picture (fig. 28).

24
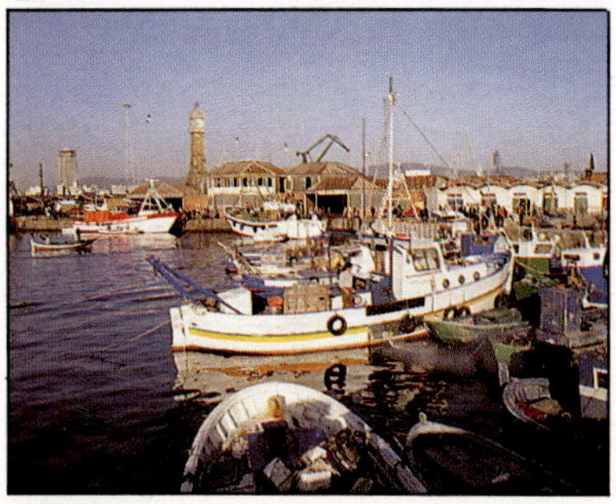

25
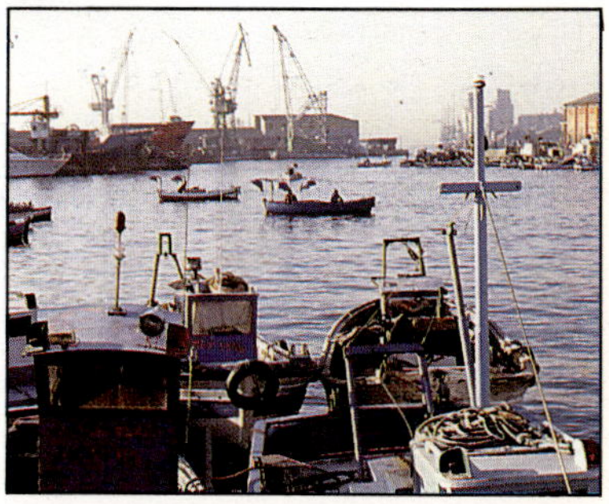

26
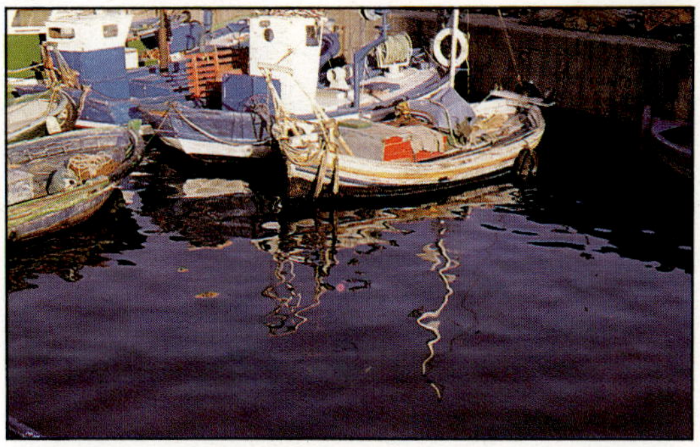

27
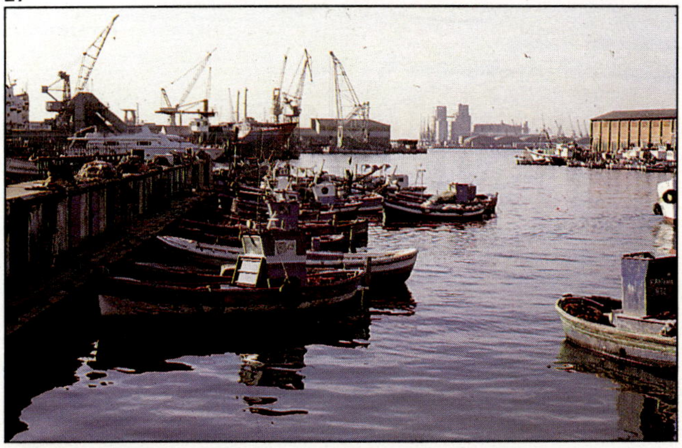

28
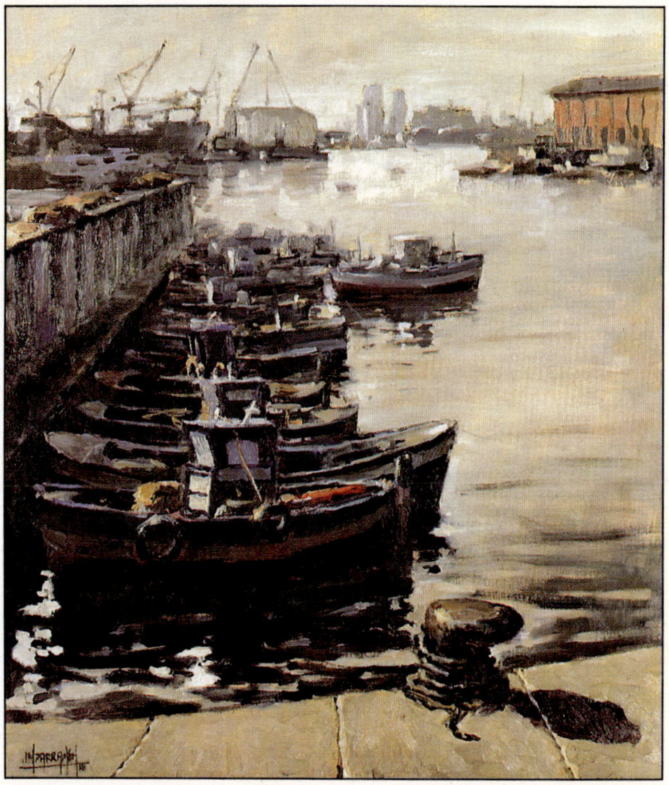

A gallery of various interpretations

29

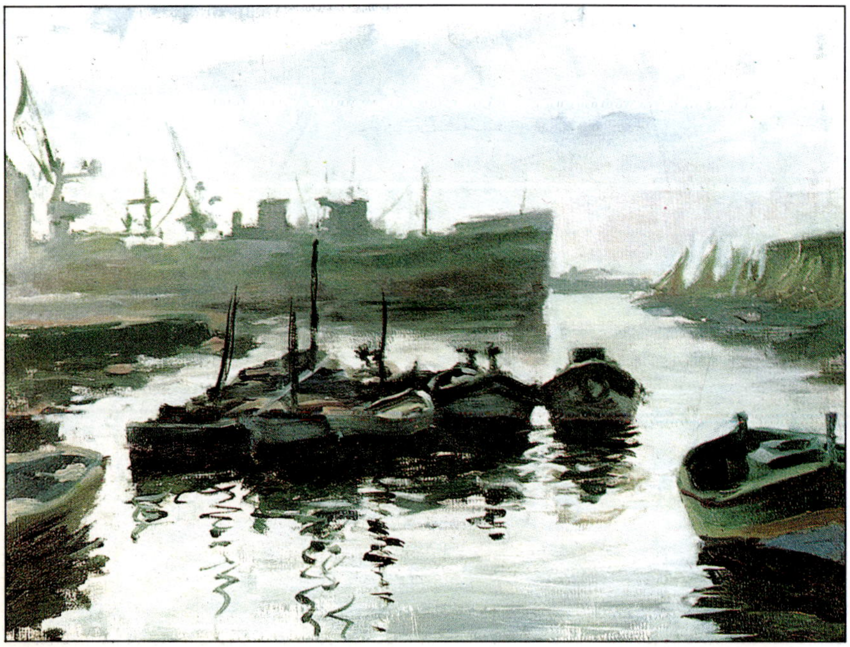

30

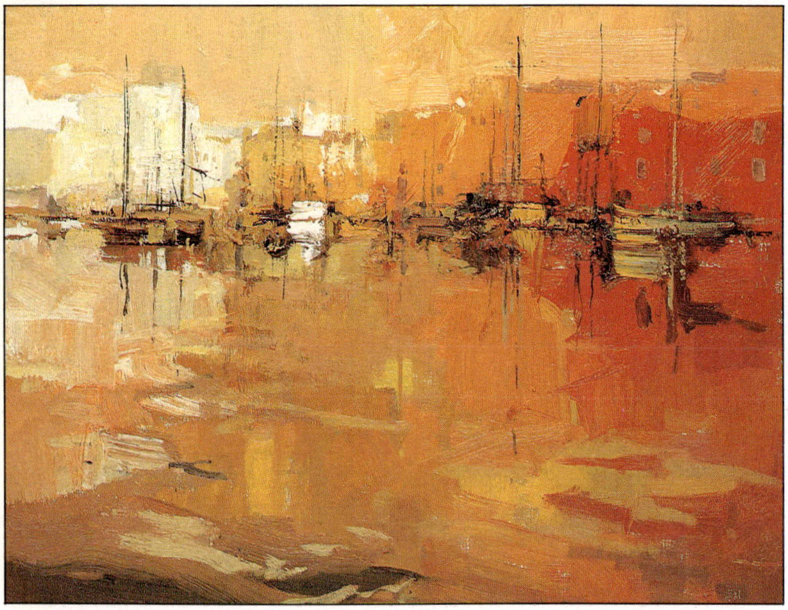

31

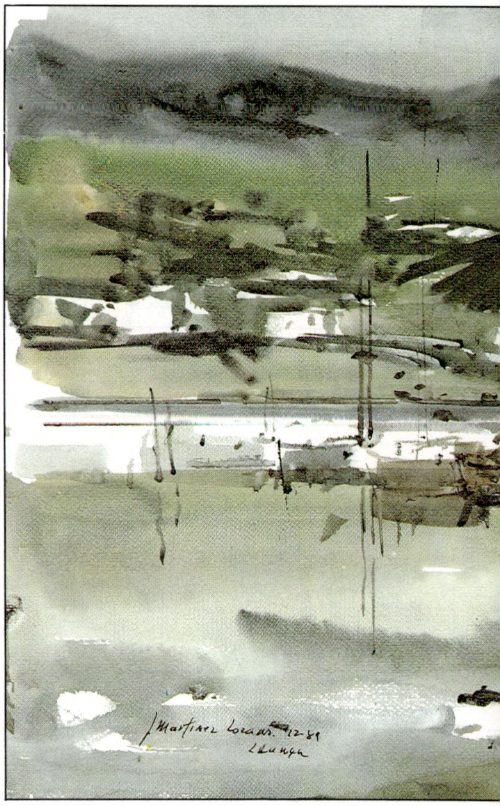

Fig. 29. There is an infinite range of possible interpretations within any given type of painting, such as the seascape. Each painter imposes his or her own personal "vision" on a theme. In this painting, J. M. Parramón expresses the variety and subtlety of the atmospheric effects inherent in this port scene.

Fig. 30. Martínez Lozano expresses exaltation by using warm, fiery colors for this scene of a northern village at dusk.

The art of painting does not just consist of applying norms or recommendations like the ones we have looked at in this short introduction. Choosing a subject using all the factors discussed here is not enough to ensure that the final result will be a work of art.

Painting is, basically, the manifestation of an "inner vision" of the world perceived by the artist, which may, according to the extent to which it affects the artist, cause him or her to alter the external reality.

In order to make effective changes, you must know about framing, various points of view, lighting, composition, and so on. You can also recall and apply any of the personal images that you have accumulated in your memory over the years. In attempting to capture your first impression of the subject, you can highlight, reinforce, reduce, or exaggerate contrasts; diminish colors or depths; or even eliminate a particular ele-

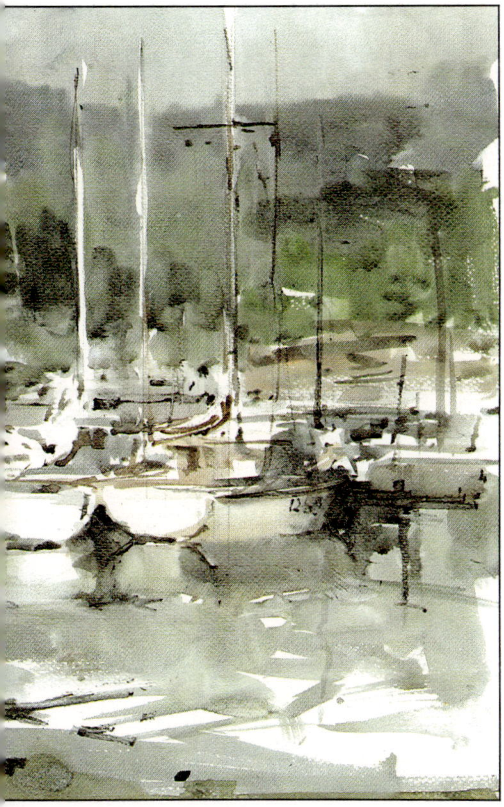

32

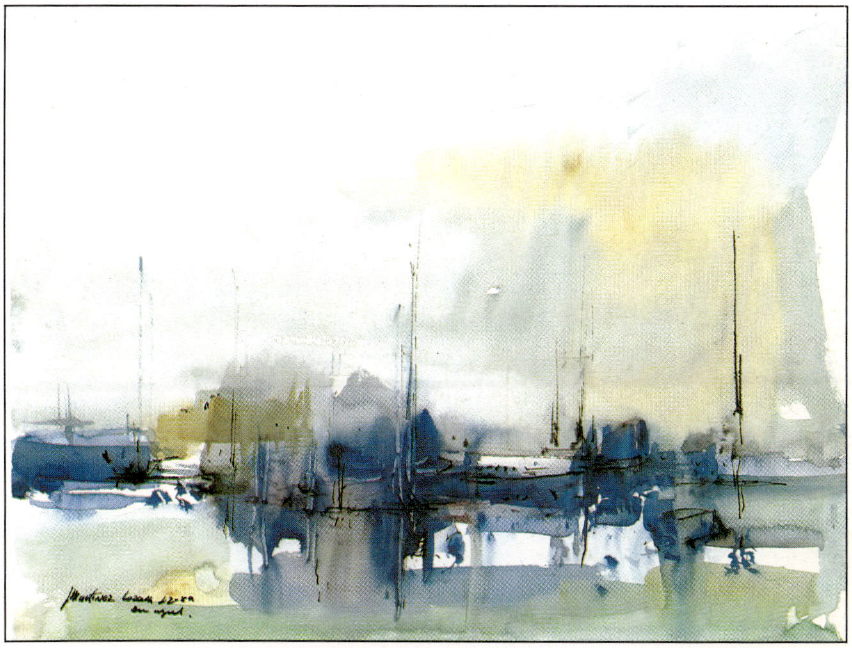

33

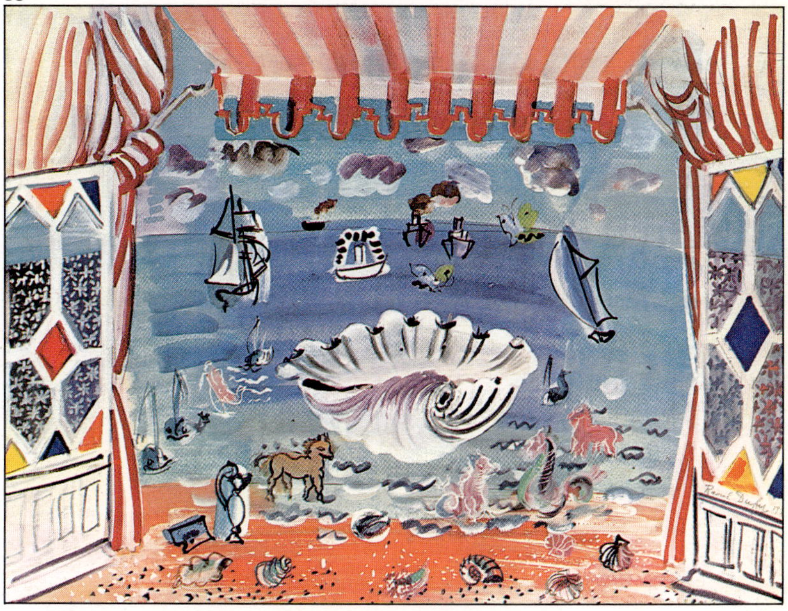

ment from your picture. You can, in essence, give free rein to your imagination and creativity. For instance, you can paint new themes or approach an old subject, such as a seascape, in different ways.

The choice of subject, in the final analysis, depends on the degree of enthusiasm and excitement that your vision of the theme inspires in you.

"We see nature as an everyday thing; the artist must see it and paint it as something fantastic and fabulous," said Marc Chagall, a true artist of interpretation.

In these pages, reproduced in figures 29 to 33, you can see some examples of the work of different artists on a similar theme, that of the seascape. The aim of these illustrations is to show you that the last word has never been said on any theme. There are always new possibilites of interpretation for any theme waiting to be discovered. From now on, the choice is yours.

Figs. 31 and 32. Various interpretations of a similar theme can be found in the work of the same artist. These two watercolors by Martínez Lozano demonstrate two different treatments of the same theme using the same technique.

Fig. 33. Raoul Dufy, *La Mediterranée*. In his desire to give free rein to his "inner vision," the artist may at times re-create the world, as it appears before him or her, in the strangest ways, evoking new, undiscovered realities.

Painting at home

34

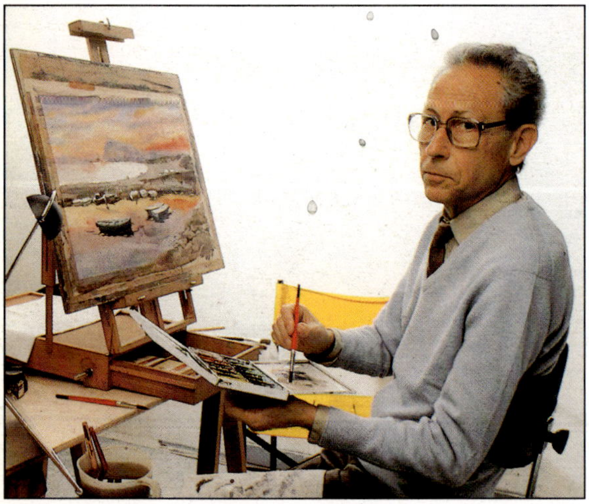

Amand Domènech is a painter who for many years was a graphic designer, which, he admits, has had a direct influence on his painting style. "Above all," he says, "on the detail and precision of my work at times." Domènech finds the studio the ideal place for him to express both influences in his painting. It is in the studio where he does most of his work.

It is at the studio of our photographer where we are going to show you the artistry of Amand Domènech. A desk with an adjustable drawing board has been set up; alongside it is a small table where the artist can keep his materials. The lighting has also been prepared beforehand. We have arranged soft lighting with uniform intensity over the whole area—"bathing" the space with light, without casting shadows.

"It is the kind of lighting we could compare to that reflected by a white wall," comments the photographer. The lighting is completed with the complementary effect of a light that reflects onto the wall.

These are, obviously, ideal conditions that have little do to with the "surprises" that painting in the open air can give. Amand Domènech, though he has experienced painting in the open air, perhaps because of his firsthand knowledge of the problems inherent at times in working outdoors, declares himself a "studio painter."

Fig. 34. Amand Domènech is a painter with years of experience behind him. He has painted both from real life in the open air and in the studio. Lately he has tended to paint less and less out-of-doors, preferring to work in the studio.

35

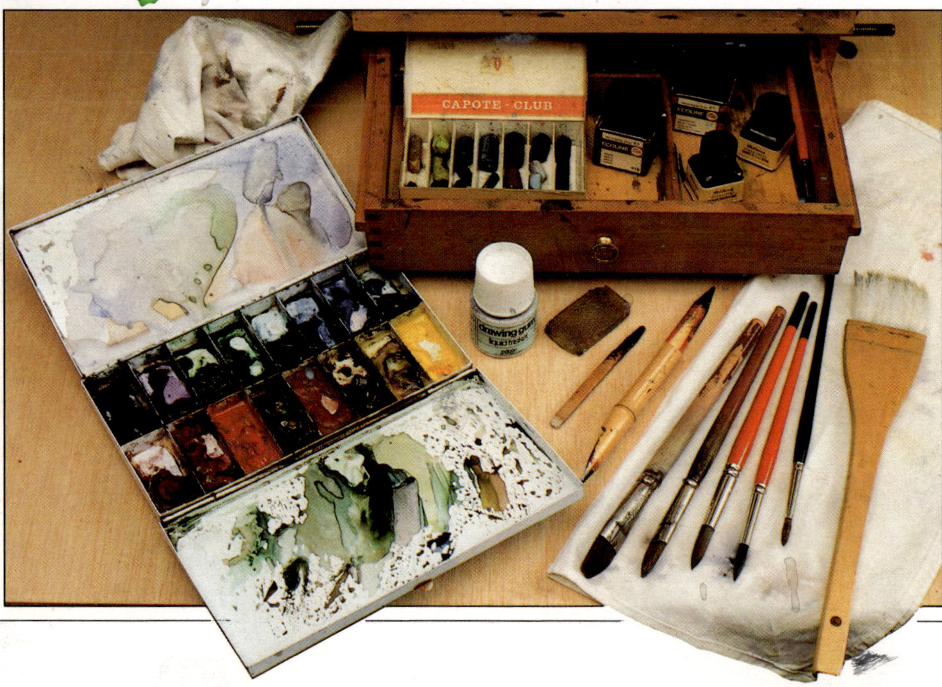

Fig. 35. Domènech generally uses Fabriano paper for watercolor painting. He normally equips himself with eleven or twelve brushes, though he does not always use them all in his work. For this picture, he has chosen two flat brushes (one of ox hair), two round brushes (a no. 7 and a no. 12), and a filbert brush. The elements that give life to his watercolor painting are ink, which he will apply with a cane, wax crayons, and a range of sixteen watercolors. The list of materials is completed by liquid frisket to save white areas, a rubber eraser, and a scalpel, which he will not use here.

The detailed paintings of Amand Domènech

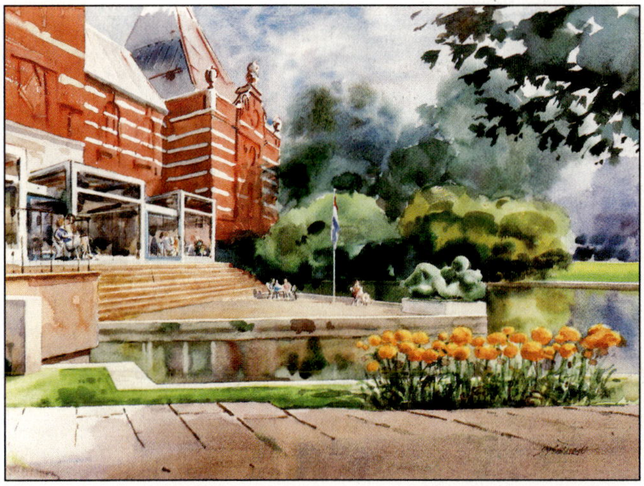

36

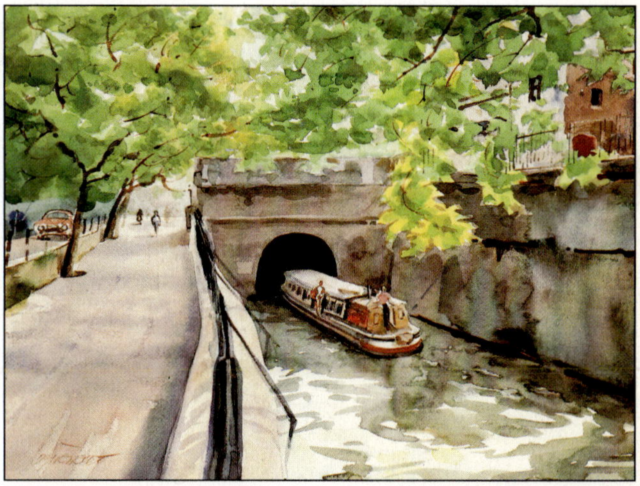

37

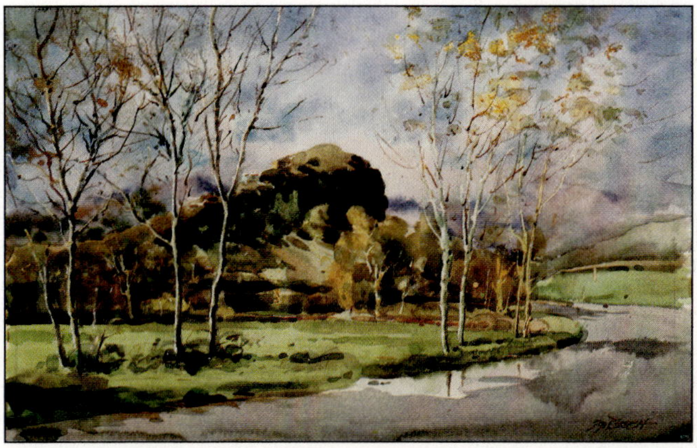

38

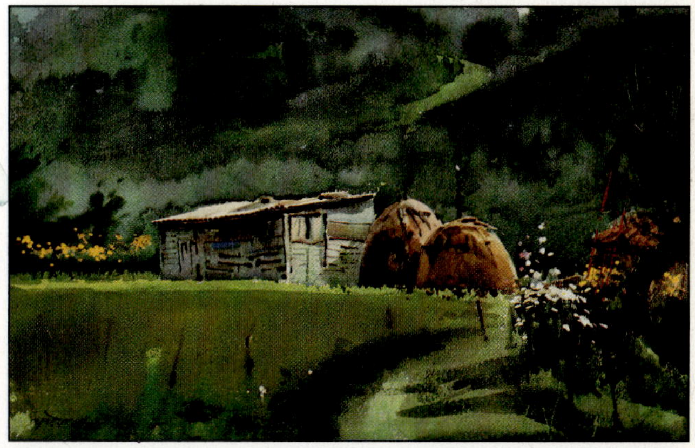

39

Figs. 36 to 40. This is just a small selection of the prolific work of Amand Domènech. Besides an evident similarity in theme—all can be considered landscapes of one type or another, urban, rural, or maritime—they all have a certain quality in common that enables the viewer to identify them as the works of the same artist. They all reveal the same control, the same urge to depict things with careful detail, whether they be a group of flowers, a quay, the leaves of a tree, or a haystack. Yet close study also reveals that the brushstrokes making up these pictures are free. The washes are full of spontaneity, confirming Amand Domènech's mastery of his profession.

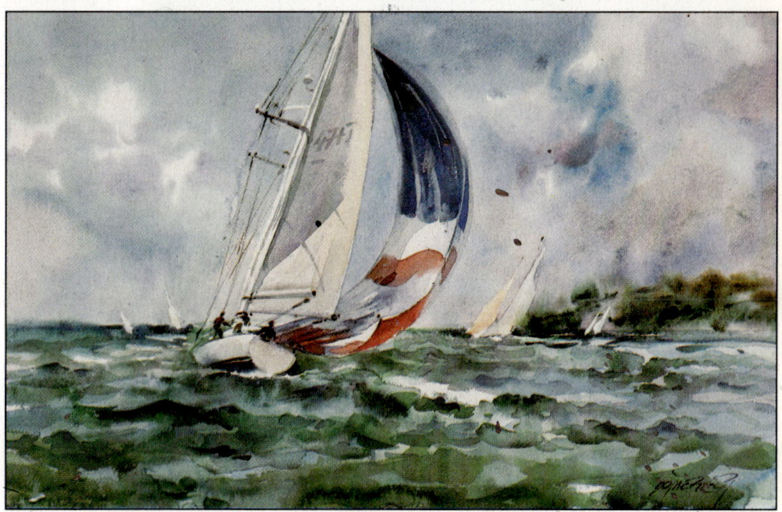

40

Step one: the preliminary base

41

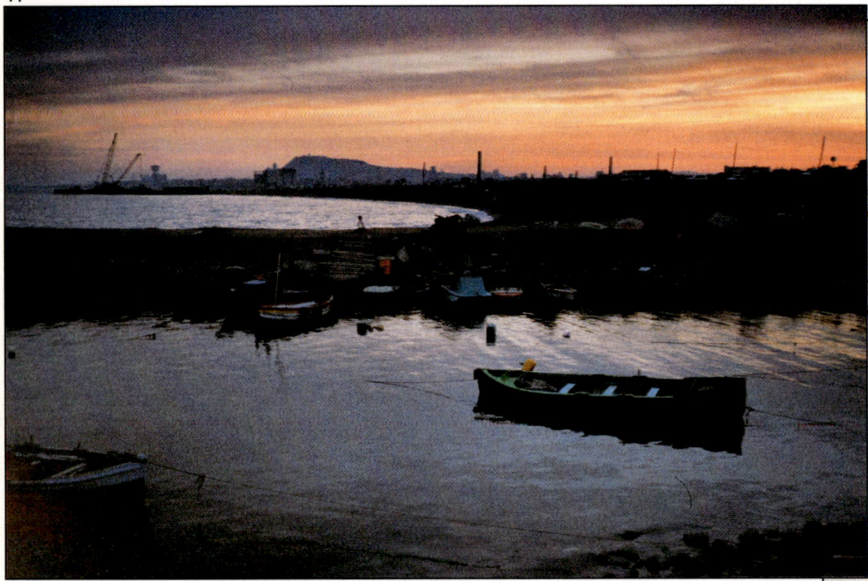

42

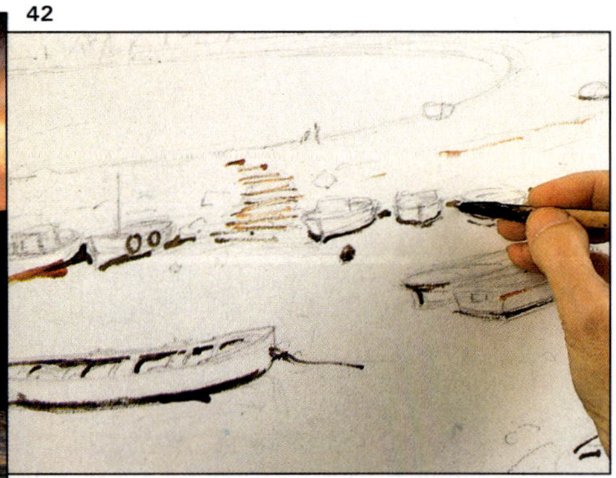

43

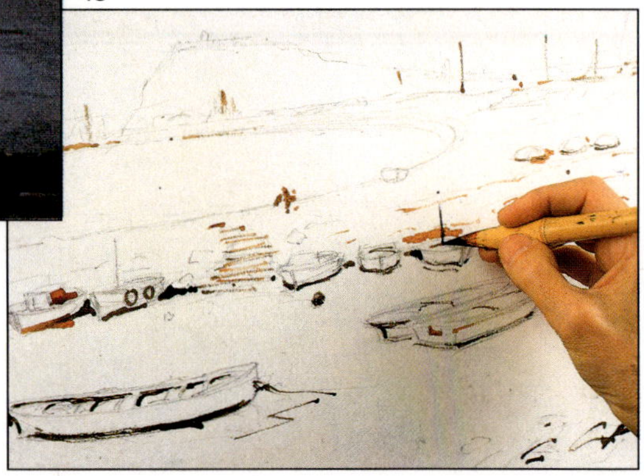

Fig. 41. Photography is a valuable medium in the work of Amand Domènech. It can retain moments that stir his imagination and emotions. Photography allows him to bring these moments into the studio. In this case, photography has also been used to capture an image, that of a sunset over the sea, which would have been practically impossible to paint there and then due to the lack of sufficient light.

Figs. 42 and 43. Preparatory work with ink and liquid watercolors, applied with a cane, is one of the highly personal techniques of this painter. Not only does this make the original drawing stand out, but it becomes the foundation for effects that enrich the finished watercolor. The artist can obtain different lines and strokes according to whether the point of the cane is thick and uneven or fine and precise. Strangely, the Japanese cane (fig. 43) is the one he uses the least. "I much prefer the other one," says Domènech. "The one which is little more than a stick."

The subject

Amand Domènech has decided to take as his subject for this seascape a small quay harboring a group of fishing vessels. The real theme of the picture, however, is the light of dusk. Notice how light and shadow form a delicate balance at this time of day.

It is a challenging undertaking. As Domènech has said, "Shadows are always difficult to get just right, even more difficult with watercolor, when you can never be sure of the results. Even though I have painted this subject before, it is challenging."

Added to these difficulties is the fact that Domènech is painting from a photograph, which makes it all the harder to capture the spontaneity of the fleeting moment he is trying to depict.

The artist arrives at the studio with his drawing of the subject practically finished. He has sketched out the basic composition of his picture giving a few suggestive lines, and has given a clear definition to the whole structure of the painting. Furthermore, he has altered the position and size of some of the boats and has "invented" others. All this is done to achieve a compositional harmony "which a photo rarely gives us," to quote Amand Domènech.

A trick of the trade

Before beginning to paint, the artist carries out what he calls his "preliminary preparation," which consists of "redrawing" certain areas of the picture with lines and ink stains.

This method, which he considers very much a part of his own personal style, enriches the quality of the actual painting. He takes a thin drawing cane dipped in sienna ink and, with a free, spontaneous hand, goes over the lines of the boats. Before making each line, he tests the thickness of each stroke in the marking of his paper to get rid of surplus ink.

He works in a very relaxed manner, changing drawing cane and ink from time to time. At times, he is very careful about how he follows a particular line on his drawing. Sometimes he inks over the drawing with a loose, freer style. Whichever way he draws, the ink, applied to the surface of this dry paper, breaks up and hardens his original lines. We can appreciate the different qualities that the cane gives to a picture,

44

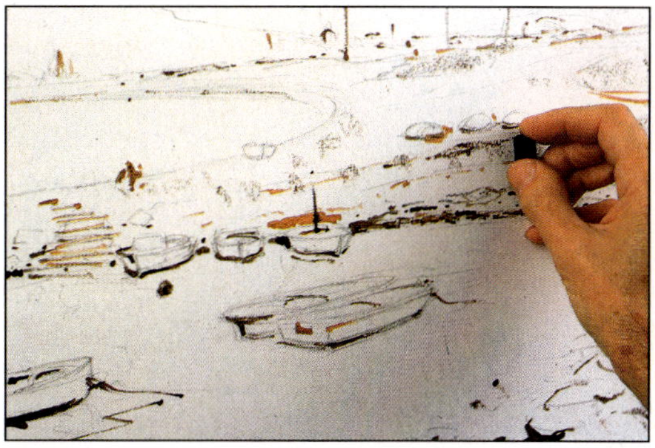

45

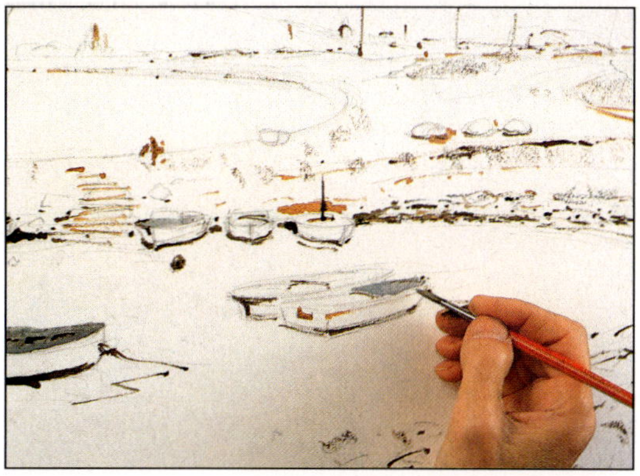

46

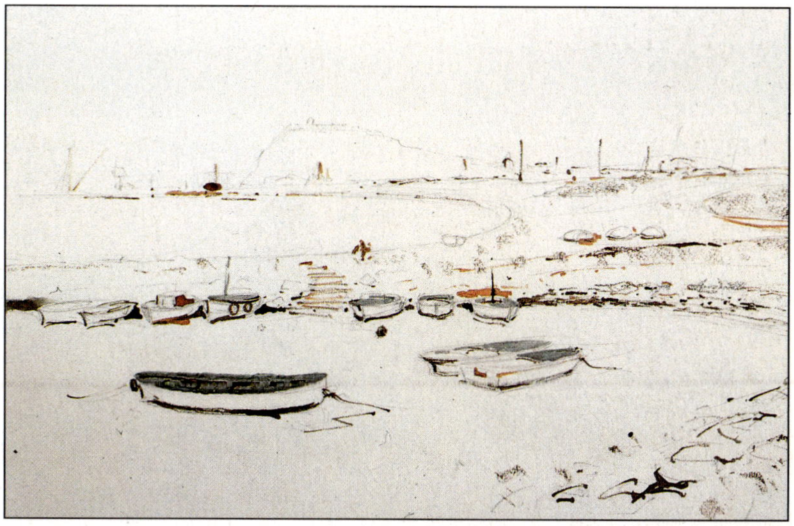

from precise, thin lines such as those produced by the Japanese cane, to the more irregular and thicker lines made by other types.

Domènech "redraws" both the towers and the cranes in the background and the rocks in the foreground. He uses the same mixture of sienna and reddish earth, drawing with both India ink and liquid watercolors. "Liquid watercolors can be mixed later with new tones when water is added," Domènech explains.

Our guest artist examines the drawing board under the light, and sees that the ink is dry enough to continue working. "Now, I'll put on a bit of wax," he says. He takes a small, flat piece of sepia-colored wax and proceeds to drag it over his paper, creating horizontal strips that will later correspond to the areas of the picture in shade. As he is working with coarse-grain watercolor paper, these stains allow the white of the paper to show through.

In this preparatory work, Domènech has laid down a base of lines and dark stains that act as "underlining" for the subsequent task of painting. Watercolor being a transparent material, everything he has done up to now will still be visible when the picture is finished.

He chooses the finest of his round brushes and begins to paint. "No, no, I'm going to paint in the reserves," he explains. To do this, he dips his brush in the bottle of liquid frisket and covers the boat on the left with it. He pauses. He lifts the drawing board closer. In this way, he can work more comfortably and achieve greater precision.

We are at a tricky moment. He outlines the insides of the boats, resting his right hand, his painting hand, on the other, as if it were a maulstick. Having completed this stage, he goes back to his usual position. Throughout this time, he never ceases to carefully study the photograph he is using as a model. He is doubtlessly trying to foresee the final results.

Now, Domènech asks for a diferent light, one that will shine directly onto the photo so that he does not have to strain his eyes to see. It really is difficult to truly re-create the quality of natural light. And, now, unfortunately, Amand Domènech has to paint without it.

Fig. 44. Domènech uses wax crayons to finish his preparatory work. A range of similar tones, sepias and siennas, help to give shape to the areas in shadow. The artist rubs them over the paper, which, being rough and still dry, allows the background to show through a little.

Fig. 45. Painting with watercolor provides a series of solutions to the problem of creating white areas, such as using liquid masks or scratching with a brush, a beveled edge, or a knife. Amand Domènech prefers using liquid frisket when reserving whites as, being clean and precise, it is more suited to his character. The method is simple, you just paint the area you wish to reserve, let it dry, and rub it off with a rubber eraser when you are ready to paint the reserve.

Fig. 46. The first stage is complete. Our artist, with his inks and wax, has produced a subtle base of lines and small stains that, as we will see later on, will play an important role in the finished picture.

Step two: painting with complementary colors

While Domènech finally prepares to start painting, he tells us about his own understanding of what painting in watercolor means: "Painting in watercolor means that you have to be able to grasp the moment, so you don't want to be interrupted." We take note of this and will do our best not to disturb him.

The artist stands up, and, after adjusting the height of the easel accordingly, he picks up the drawing board and paper, and places it at one end of the table. With the priming brush dipped in water, he wets the top part of the paper, the sky, down to where it ends on the horizon. As his brushstrokes cover the paper, we see how the previously applied light touches of ink and watercolor begin to spread and soften.

Over this wet base, which will allow him to soften any color he paints over it, Domènech starts to paint the sky. He takes his flat brush and mixes yellow with a little carmine on this palette, obtaining a soft orange color, which he then proceeds to apply in long brushstrokes from left to right. After this, he stains the adjoining areas with a violet tone. These orange-yellow and violet-blue colors are thought of as complementary and therefore give striking contrast to the picture. With complementary colors, Domènech intends to depict the fiery sky that dominates the picture.

Domènech continues painting. Soon, tones that are related to the two basic colors of the picture are added; they enrich the painting, giving it a wider variety of tones. Reds and blues are gradually transformed into a range of interconnected colors, which are the result of irregular brushstrokes that gain their unity from the direction in which Domènech always paints, from left to right.

Figs. 47 to 50. Amand Domènech starts painting the sky. First he wets his paper before painting (fig. 47). This is a wet-on-wet technique, which is ideal for stumping outlines and avoiding problems such as stains of different colors (fig. 48). To depict the fiery light of dusk in this watercolor, Domènech juxtaposes complementary colors, yellow and violet (fig. 49). This brings out the full effect of the sky. His colors run freely on the paper, in a variety of patterns, toward the horizon. But, Amand Domènech applies rhythm and direction in his brushstrokes to unify the overall effect (fig. 50).

47

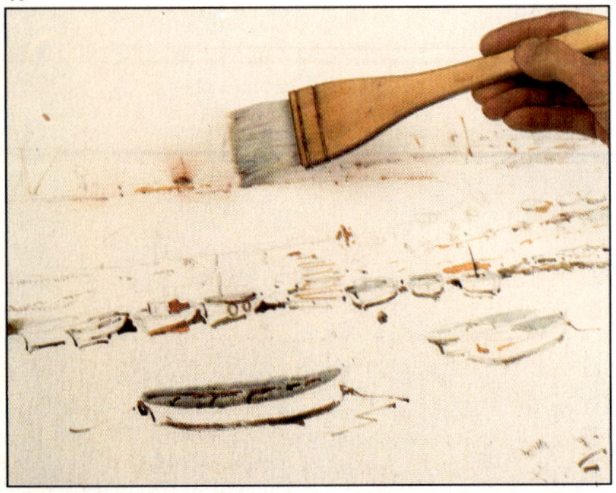

48

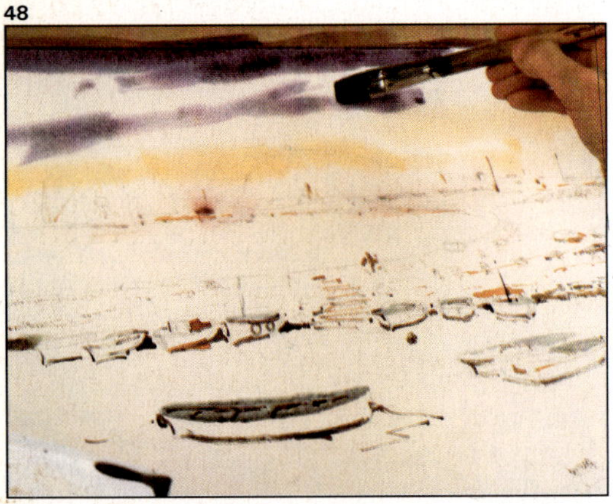

49

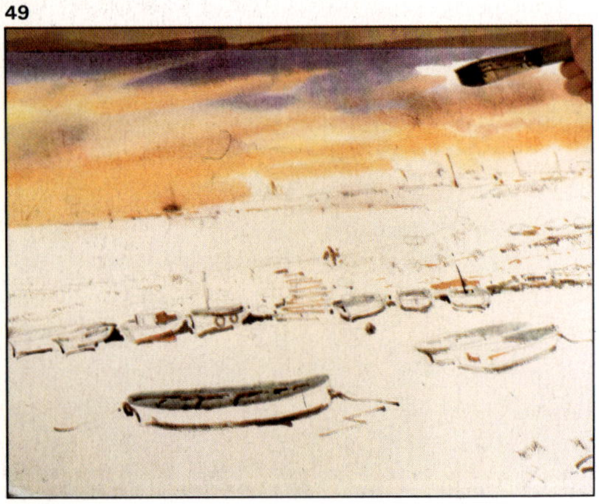

50

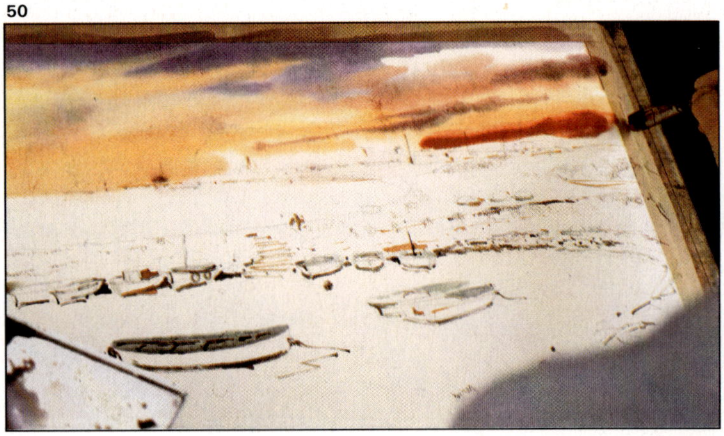

Figs. 51 to 53. The artist begins to paint the horizon over the background of the sky. He uses a very light wash that allows the layer underneath to breathe. In figures 52 and 53, you can see the effect produced by painting over a wet base. At first, the blue line of the horizon is clearly defined, but then it spreads and softens. The horizon serves as a transitional area between the sky and the sea in the distance.

Fig. 54. The sky is usually an important element in a seascape. Here, besides occupying a large area of the paper, its coloring also gives it great impact. The situation and quality of the sky as the most distant and undefined element in the picture allows the painter more freedom of interpretation. Probably, all these factors explain why Domènech chose to paint the sky first.

While painting the sky, Domènech tries out each color in the margin of glued paper that borders his watercolor. He also removes excess paint from his brush in the margin. With a violet similar to the one he used for the sky, Domènech shapes a mountain that rises over the horizon. He actually paints and draws it at the same time, with short brushstrokes that allow the warm, luminous base of the sky to show through.

To complete this stage, he adds a little more carmine to the violet and paints the horizon line, separating the sky and the sea, though not too rigidly. He allows a certain continuity between the two, as you can see in the detail reproduced in figure 53.

In this way, Amand Domènech, using the technique known as wet on wet, has managed to suggest the feeling of atmosphere and space that the horizon inspires in us.

"The sky and the middle ground," Domènech explains, "are what give greater spontaneity. Once you've defined it, you can't go over it again."

51

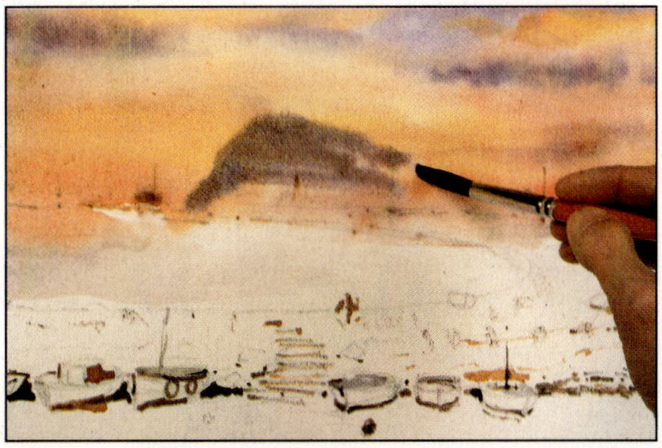

52

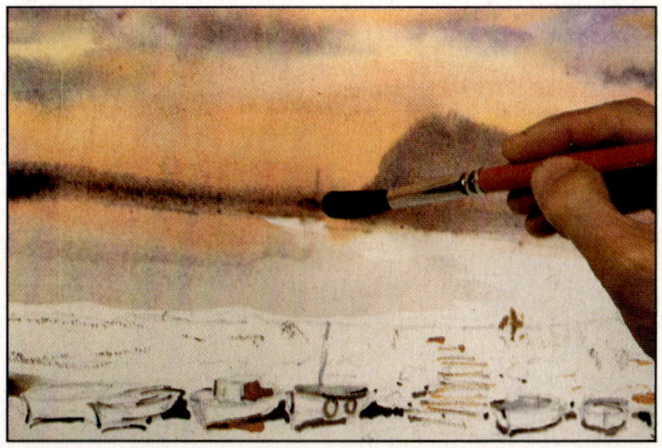

53

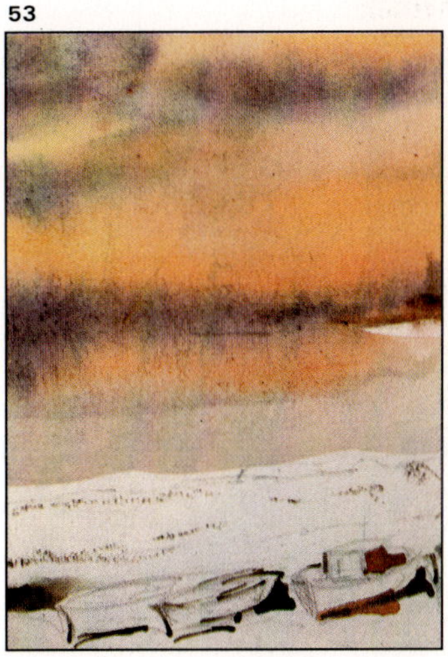

54

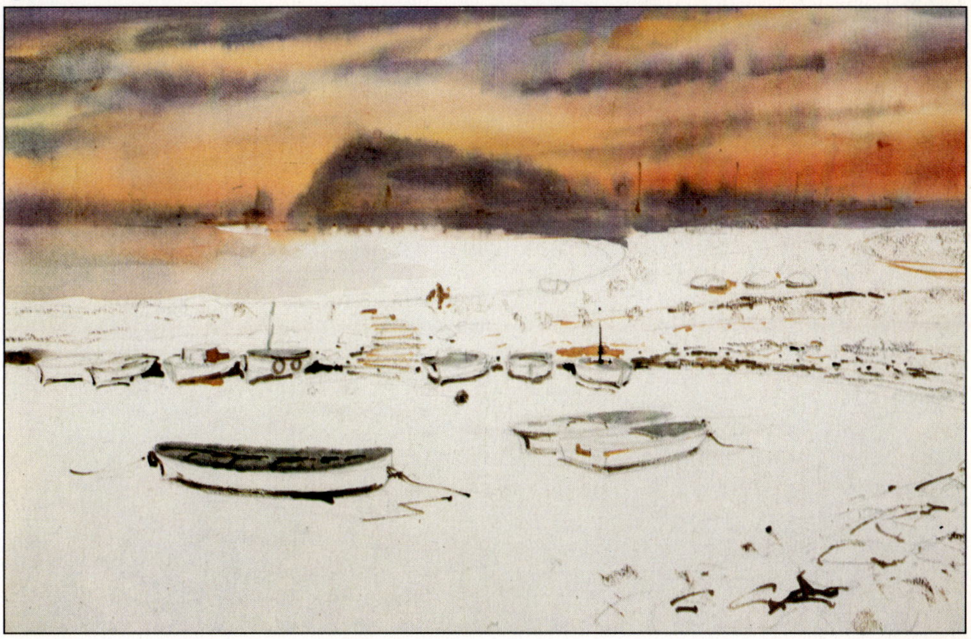

Step three: "The work of years..."

Amand Domènech decides to let the painting dry a little before continuing to paint—to avoid the excessive wetness of the paper that may make his colors run. Meanwhile, he gathers his thicker brushes as these are the ones he will use for the next stage of painting. "Someone could buy this book and think they can learn everything straight away," he comments. "But all this is the work of years."

Although Domènech is right, you should not be discouraged. The most important thing is to start working. He starts to paint again. Returning to the horizon, he emphasizes the central area with a darker brushstroke dipped in violet; this creates a subtle transition zone between the background and the area he will now begin to work on.

to capture the irregular effect of the shadows on the surface of the sea.

Amand Domènech feels that this is the time to pause to take a careful look at his work. "I mustn't torture the painting by going at it too much," he says. "This gentle rhythm is the way I usually work in the studio."

The artist uses this brief pause to clean his palette and to prepare a soft orange tone with the flat brush. He uses this color to paint the upper part of the sea in the foreground, making the colors he uses here correspond with the colors of the sky that are reflected in the sea.

As his brushstrokes descend, covering the rest of the sea, this orange tone becomes darker. Its color changes slightly.

Fig. 55. Once again, painting wet on wet, Domènech reinforces the background, suggesting the buildings that in real life appear on the horizon with a number of blue stains.

Fig. 56. He gradually approaches the foreground. The middle ground, or transition zone, the beach, is depicted with a large, warm, grayish stain in which a few small white areas have been left.

55

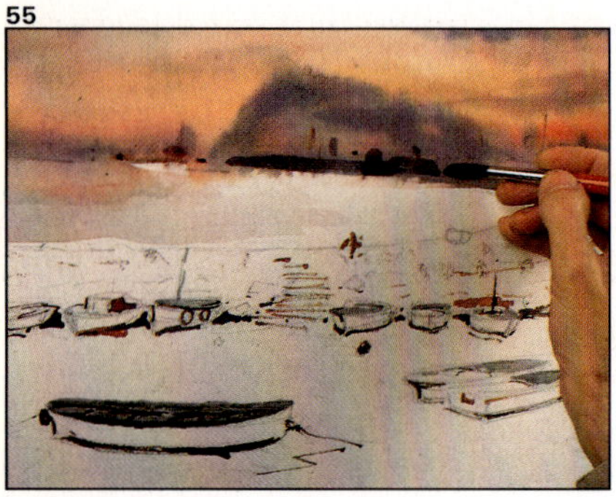

56

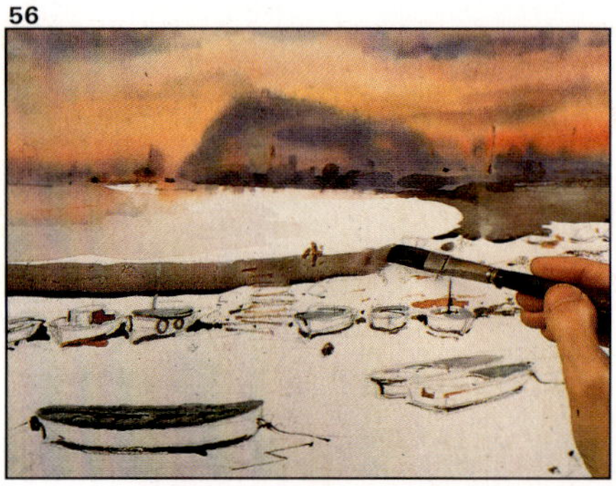

57

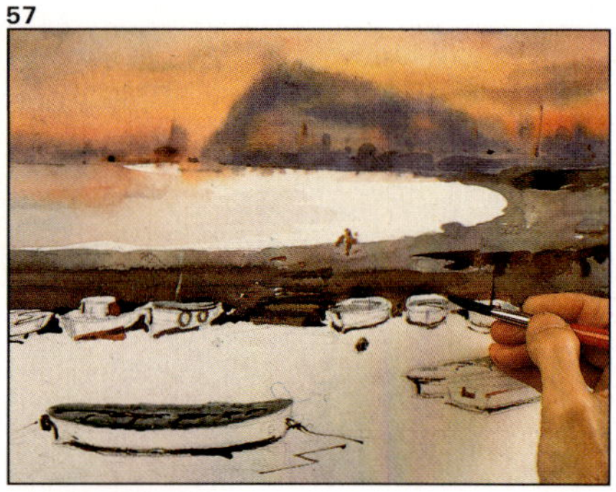

Next, he mixes a warm, broken tone on his palette, using a little sienna and Payne's gray. With this grayish color, he covers the central area of the picture, the beach. (The only part he leaves white is what will later be the boats.) This is not a completely homogenous tone. It is tinged with a touch of red to make it more earthy, and with blue and violet to make it darker. With these slight variations, Domènech "models" this section of his picture, which is not a flat area, but is slightly uneven.

Now, as the paint dries and loses its shine, you can see how the ink lines and stains drawn during the preliminary stage enhances the watercolor. The whole picture is enriched; Domènech now darkens the broken tone he is using as a base with sienna and carmine, and paints the quay. His strokes are now frenetic, zigzagging. He is seeking

58

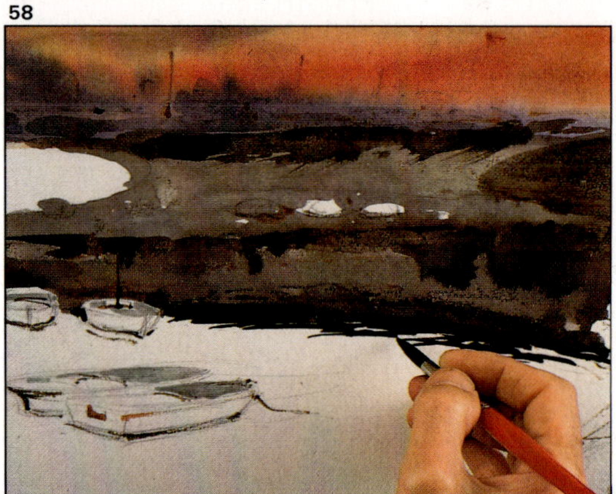

Fig. 58. Now it is time to paint the quay, certainly the darkest area of the subject. Nevertheless, Domènech, following his instincts, plays down the scarcity of light and makes the overall effect a lighter one. He paints the initial shadows on the water with a very dark tone which, by contrast, gives everything around it a lighter feeling.

Fig. 57. If you look at the photograph reproduced on page 18, you will see that the uniform grayish color of the middle ground has a delicate variety of tones that give relief and volume to the area formed by the beach. Domènech has noted this, and has accordingly darkened some areas by mixing his grayish color with a little blue and violet.

Fig. 59. Water is another central theme of the seascape. As it is a surface that reflects the light, you have to bear in mind that its appearance should have some relation with whatever it reflects.

Figs. 60 and 61. Working with too much water can sometimes present difficulties. A run can suddenly appear on the paper, ruining your work. When this happens, you must act quickly and resolutely to minimize the consequences. As you can see in the detail reproduced in figure 61, Domènech has managed to clean the brownish run that caught him by surprise.

First with carmine and later with the gradual addition of more blue, Domènech obtains a gradation of colors that ranges from warm oranges and yellows to purples and a cool violet.

Domènech allows his paint to run fairly freely, but only up to a certain point. He doesn't want the paint to accumulate too much, causing drips or abrupt edges from the previous dried colored wash. These things do happen from time to time, however, but if steps are quickly taken they are easily remedied by doing what Domènech does with an accidental run of paint (fig. 60). You just absorb the excess paint with the brush and then, wetting the brush, spread the stain over the paper, making it blend in with the picture. The main thing is that this has to be done quickly and decisively.

Domènech finishes this stage of his work by painting in the rocks in the foreground on the left, using burnt sienna. As you can see in figure 61, he works with just one brush and one color, as if it were a wash. To avoid monotony, he applies different intensities and transparencies of the color, supplementing the variety already provided by his earlier inkwork.

59

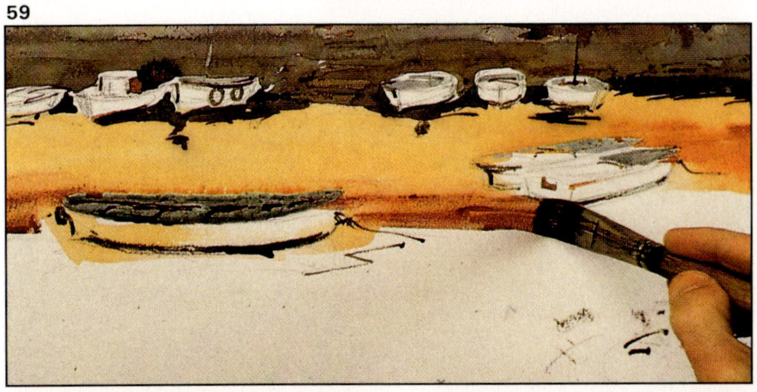

60

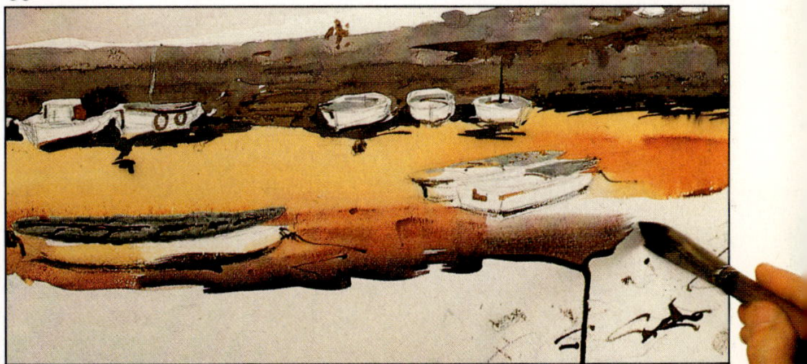

61

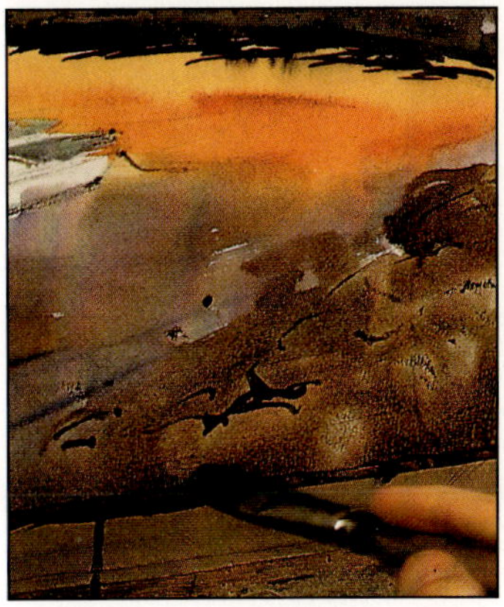

62

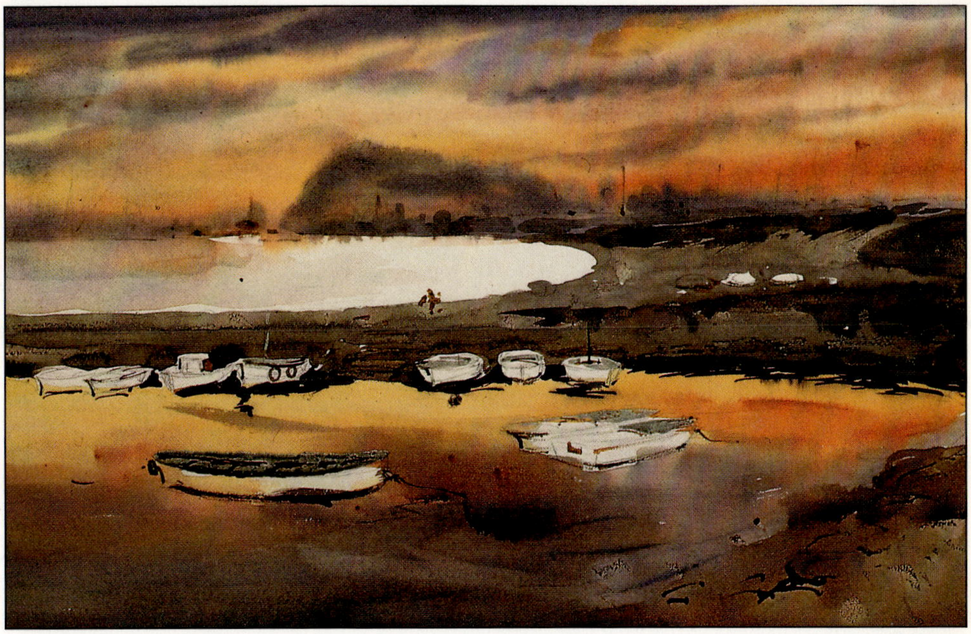

Fig. 62. The overall harmonization of the painting has been achieved. The general effect of the picture is soft, with neutral, umber and gray, tones combining with the controlled brilliance of the sky and the sea.

Step four: shadows and reflections

Amand Domènech again adjusts the height of the easel to work more comfortably. Then, he starts to paint the boats with a bottle green he has prepared. First, he paints the hull of the boat in the middle of the picture. His brushstroke is firm and decisive, but always within the limits imposed by the lines of the drawing. This insistence on quality is a feature of his work, which he acquired in his years as a graphic designer.

He paints the other boats in the same way, adding a touch of blue to his green to darken it. At the same time, he paints both the volume of the boats and the irregular shapes of the shadows they cast onto the surface of the water. Due to their undefined shape, he paints the shadows with frenetic, jumpy strokes. At first, the colors of the boats and the shadows seem to blend, as he has used practically the same tone for both. But the transparency of the watercolor soon allows the "strategically placed" ink lines drawn by Domènech from the start to show through. This is a fine example of what it means to really know your trade. "It's the work of years," as our artist would say.

Fig. 63. Little by little, the boats are all painted. Domènech interprets them as a series of lines and stains. Occasionally he uses a broken tone with a red tendency; other times he uses a cleaner color, such as this bottle green.

Fig. 64. Domènech paints with great attention to detail and order, one thing at a time. As a result, his watercolor makes rather slow progress. He takes time to think out each brushstroke.

63

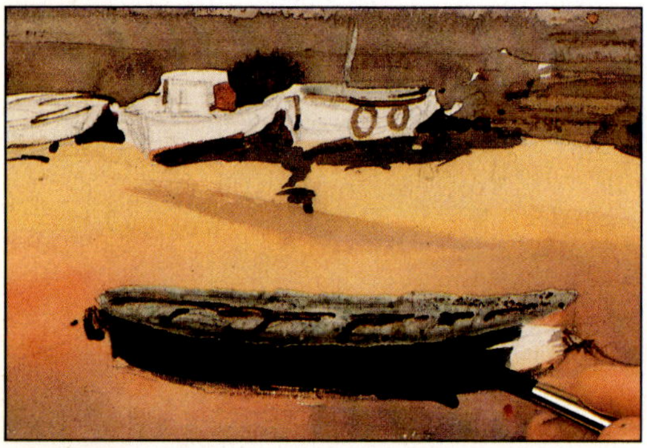

64

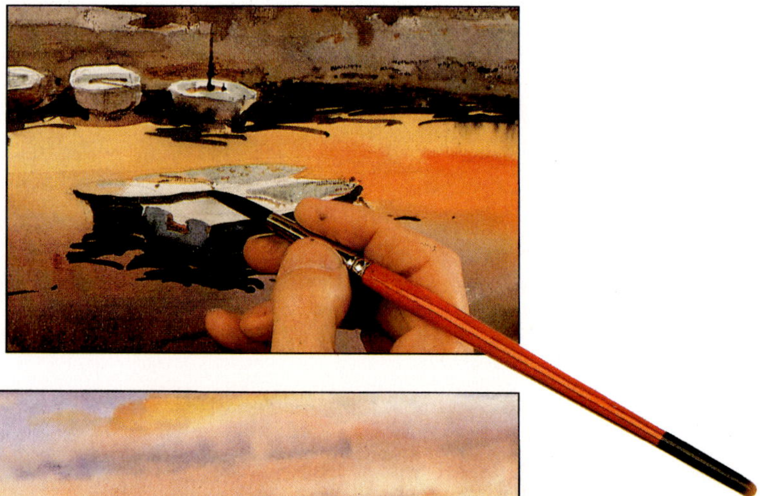

65

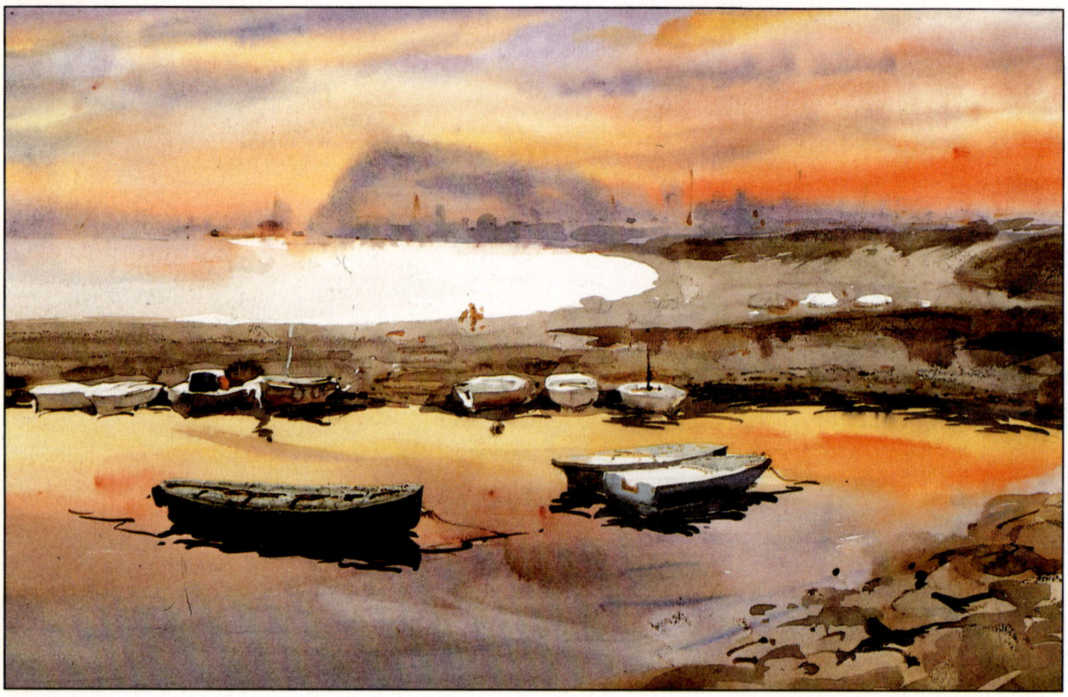

Fig. 65. Now, he paints over the rocks in the foreground once more. With the same sienna, he paints the central area of the beach, combining definitive brushstrokes—similar to the way he painted the sky—with brushstrokes that bring out transparent effects. He then allows his picture to dry a little to avoid excessive wetness.

Step five: the tones of the sea

Figs. 66 to 68. These three illustrations show in detail how Domènech has used different tones on the sea. Earlier, we saw him painting the base. He will now paint over this area. This base has to be dry enough so that the ultramarine blue and carmine he now applies (figs. 66 and 67) do not mix with the warmer colors below. In figure 68, he uses only an orange-tinged wash, painting in different tones in just one stroke.

With his palette clean once more, Domènech prepares a violet tone by mixing ultramarine blue and carmine to use on the area of sea nearest to us to complete his painting. The painter covers the base with thick strokes of a flat brush, zigzagging from left to right. Since the base is quite dry, the new color is the result of a layering of colors. Colors that, despite the overall uniformity of tone, provide a wide range of hues, some warm and full of light, others cool and duller.

Now, he changes brushes. He chooses a round brush to paint the more distant area of sea with the same violet color. He stains only the left-hand section, leaving the other side white for the time being. This area will provide a gradual transition to the more luminous area of the sea, which will be painted with a very fine, delicate orange.

66

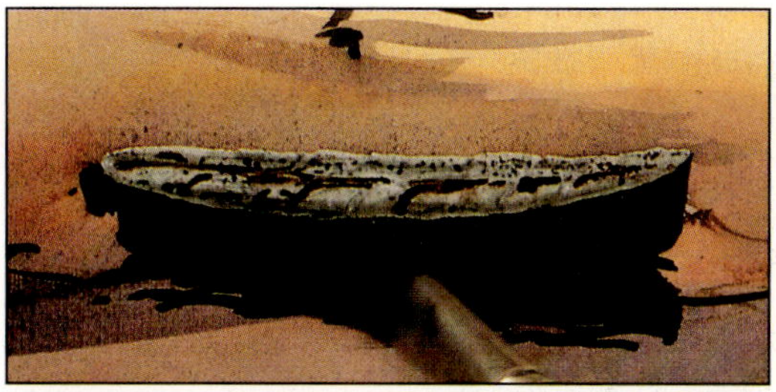

67

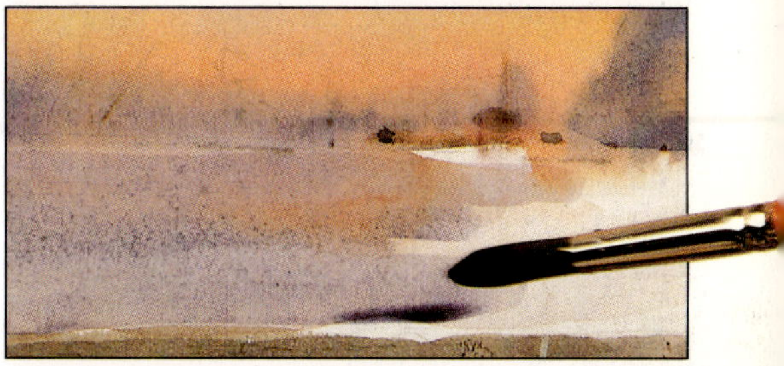

68

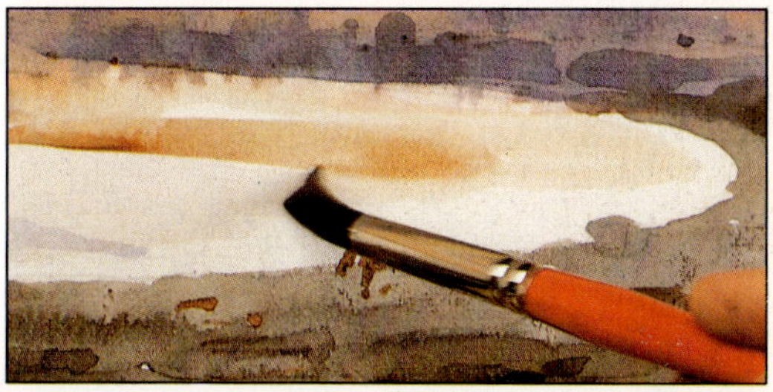

69

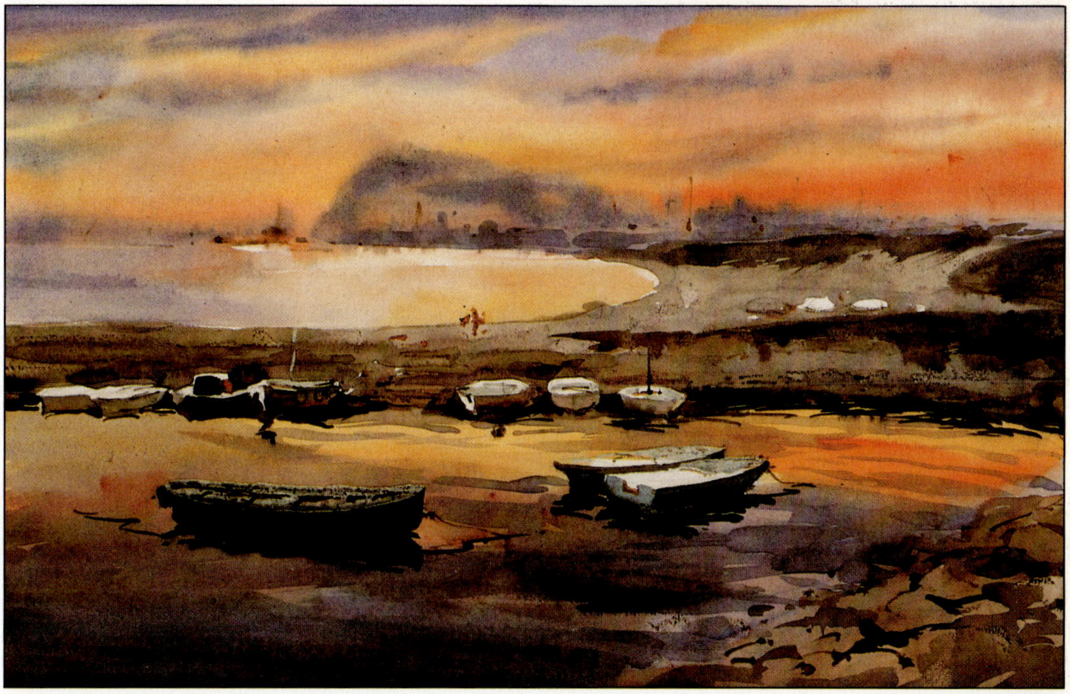

Fig. 69. Compare this picture with figure 65 on the previous page. You can see that the picture has progressed according to the design of the artist.

Step six: finishing touches

70

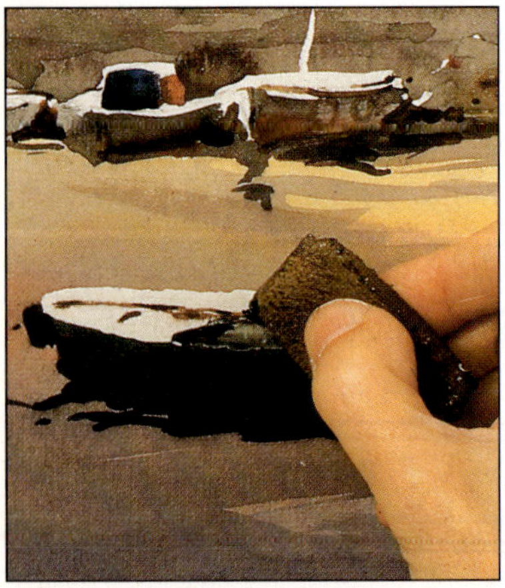

71

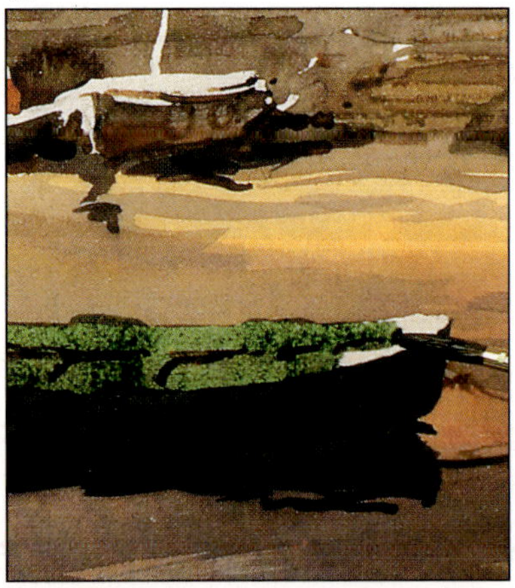

Fig. 70. Amand Domènech uses a rubber eraser to remove the liquid frisket. He reveals a perfectly shaped white area.

Fig. 71. To finish, Domènech carefully paints the whites with lively colors such as green, blue, and sienna—colors that correspond to the boats.

73

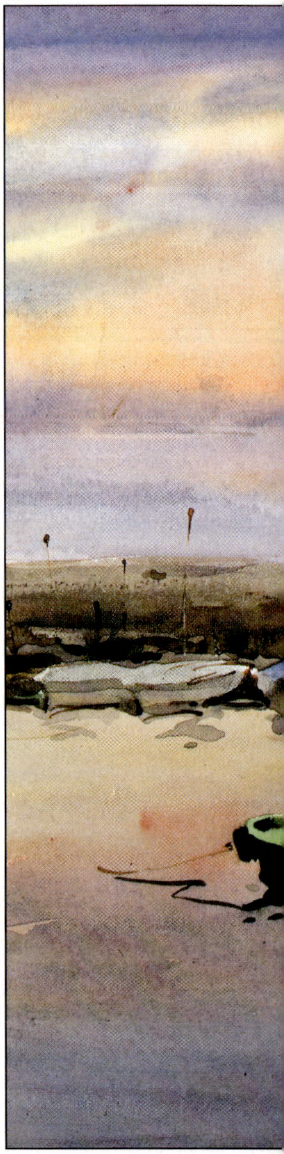

72

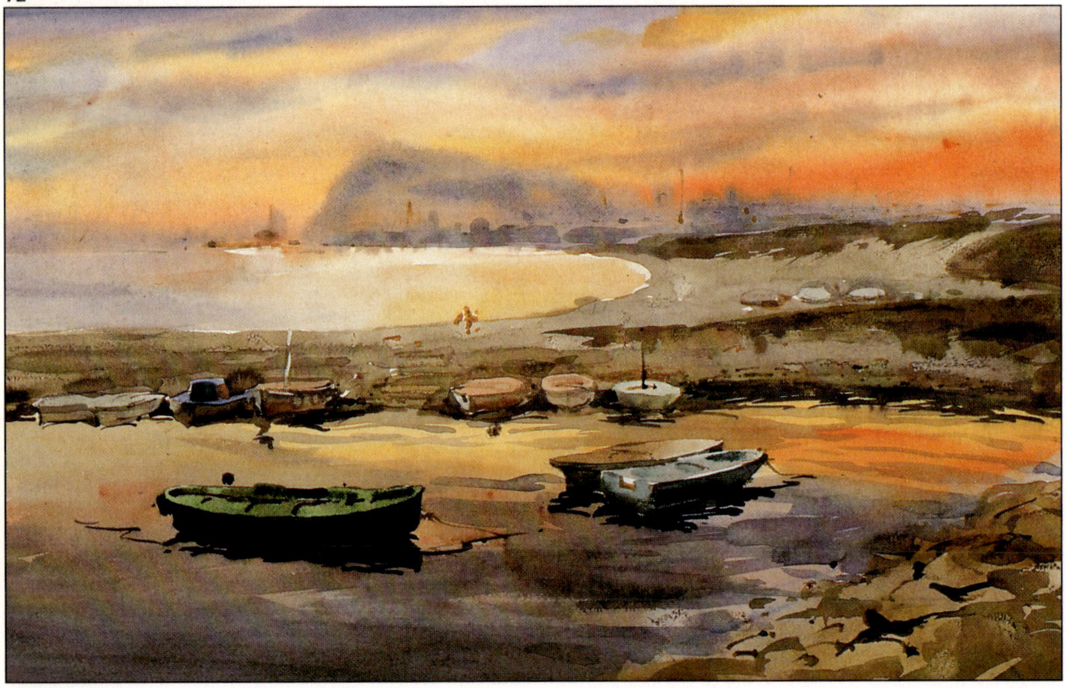

The session has slowly advanced to the stage where just a few finishing touches remain to be added. In Domènech's opinion, this stage is the most important and the most educational part of his work. He has made it clear from the start that he wanted to paint something for us that would be of the most educational value possible. In this stage, he is concerned with "staining the whites," which remain in the boats, and one or two other elements. Domènech says, he will "finish up in the studio, taking my time."

For the moment, he is going to remove the reserves he left in the boats. To do this, he begins rubbing those areas with a hard eraser, and the reserves remove easily. Domènech really didn't need to use the liquid frisket to reserve the whites; he could have used a wax pencil or simply painted with the utmost care not to cover these sections. But, Domènech says, "That would have been unnatural for me. What it comes down to is everybody's personal idea of what painting is."

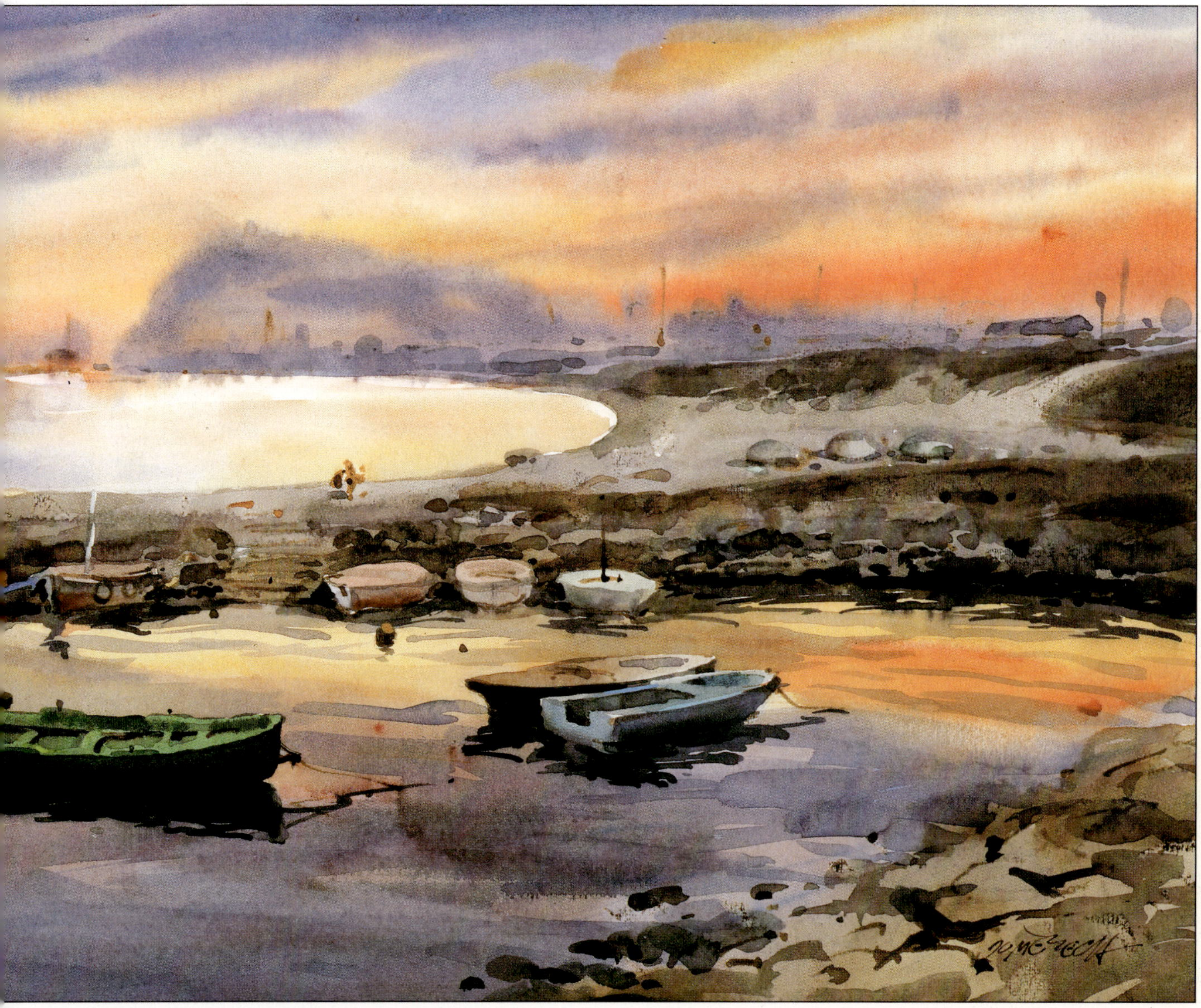

No matter what the best method may be, you have to admit that the results of the one the painter has used in this case are excellent. The white patches have been left completely clean.

Domènech now "kills off" these whites, using colors that correspond to each boat, but shinier. Green, blue, sienna, and sepia finally cover the last remaining traces of white paper, and the painting is finished.

Figs. 72 and 73. Although these two pictures may seem almost identical at first glance, you should not be deceived. If you look closely, you will observe small details—the results of work in the studio.

Domènech has darkened the central area with a light wash of Payne's gray and sepia. As a result, he was able to accentuate the various tones in the picture without weakening the impact of the central focus of his painting—the fiery color of the sea.

The artist and his materials

74

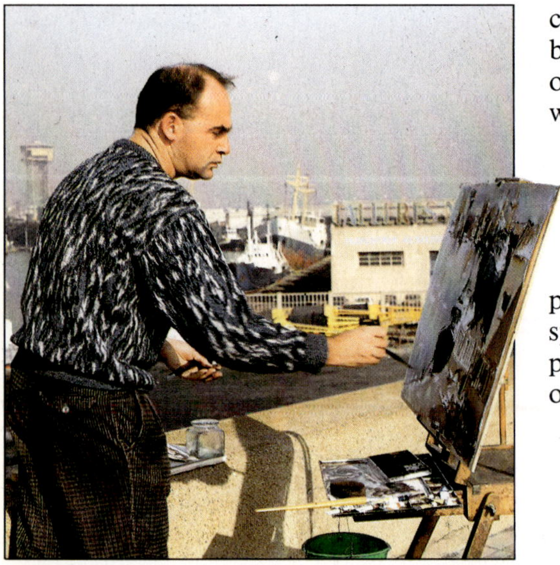

Right from the first moment of meeting Manel Plana, you feel that you are in the presence of a most unusual painter. Both his character and his magnificent work, which we have been lucky enough to be able to see in his studio, contribute to this impression. Plana is amiable and open to suggestions, though he may not accept all of them. His ideas are clear, which his work verifies.

His prolific work, which he has presented at many exhibitions and painting competitions, ranges from landscapes and seascapes to still lifes, figures, and even animals.

All his works, whether in oil or watercolor, are painted with the same characteristic light, loose touch.

Manel Plana always takes great care over the preparation of his materials for painting. To paint for us, he gathers together the following materials, which can be seen in figures 75 and 76:

A folding wooden drawing board, measuring 19½"×27½" (50×70 cm), which he made himself.

A folding easel with a built-in metal palette for mixing watercolors.

Two fairly broad *petit-gris*-hair (typically French wash brushes, of squirrel's hair) filbert brushes, a no. 4 and a no. 8; two round no. 10 and no. 4 brushes, of the same class of hair; and a couple of sow-hair brushes, tough and much-used, generally for oil painting, and hardly ever for painting in watercolor.

Various tubes of paint: cadmium yellow, orange, garanza violet (similar to carmine or magenta), burnt sienna, ultramarine blue, and indigo.

He has two sheets of 300-gr. Whatman paper, 27½"×25½" (70×65 cm); a sponge, broken into two halves; a small plastic pot for water; and a plastic bottle full of water.

Fig. 74. Manel Plana is a tireless worker who lives only to paint. Despite this, he does not mind showing us the "tricks" of his trade.

Fig. 75. Plana believes that materials are there to serve the painter. At times, he makes his own tools. For example, to paint on large sheets of paper, he built his own foldable drawing board, which you see the back of in this illustration.

75

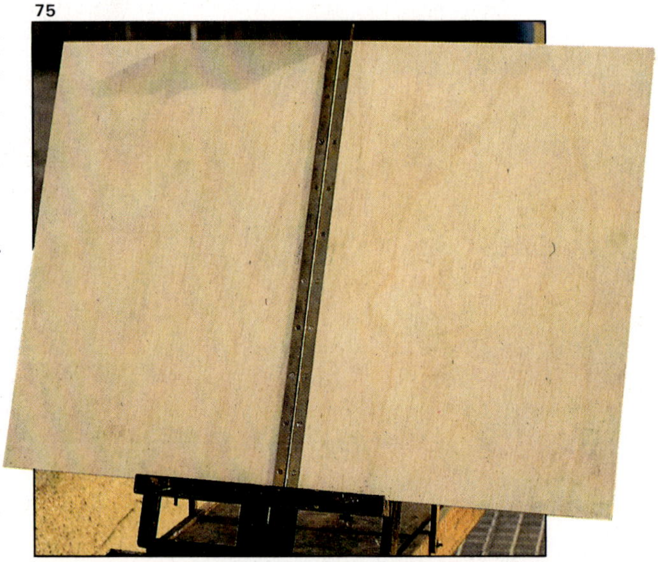

76

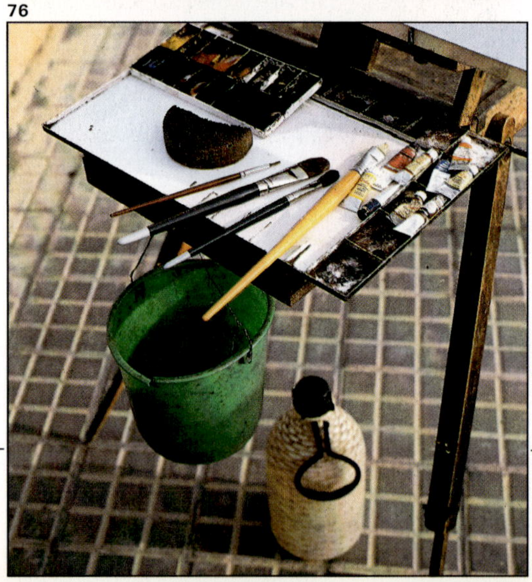

Fig. 76. The rest of his equipment is basically made up of a large metal palette and a small metal box where he keeps his paints. He usually works with just a few brushes, dipping them into the bucket he always keeps close at hand, hanging from his easel.

Light, the outstanding feature in the work of Manel Plana

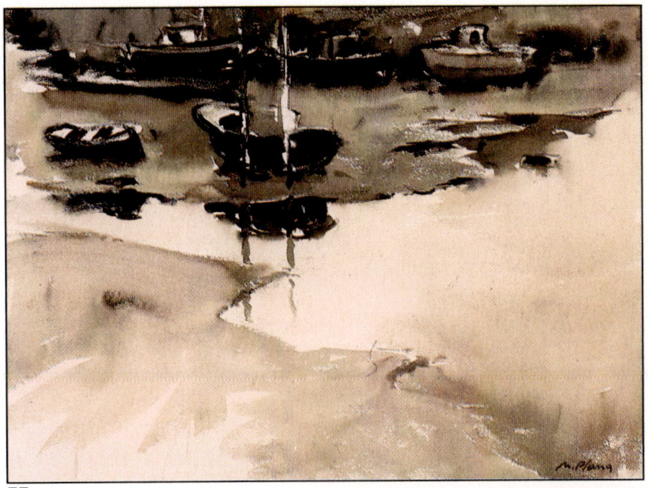

77

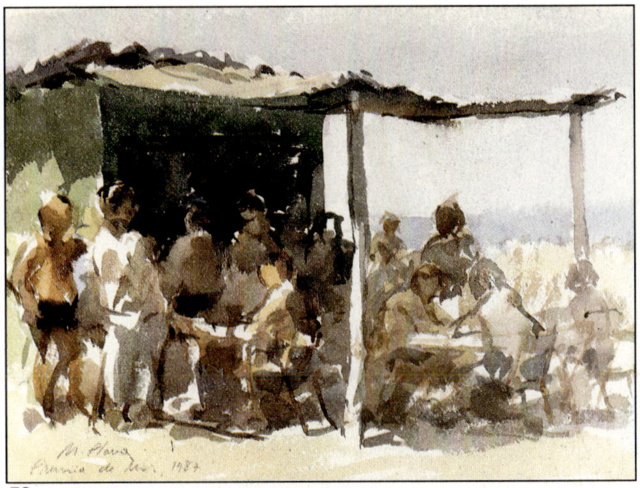

78

Figs. 77 to 79. Light is, without a doubt, the principal element in the work of Manel Plana. Light that is captured and transmitted to the canvas or paper with an enviable mastery of synthesis and speed. Most of Plana's paintings contain a highly defined, fairly limited color range, but a range that contains a rich variety of tones, as you can see in figure 77. The artistry in his brushstrokes can convert the most everyday scenes into suggestive, attractive pictures. For example, a boisterous group of people sheltering themselves from the burning sun under the shade of a beach hut becomes the perfect subject for working on problems of light and shade, as well as forms and colors (fig. 78). Manel Plana also uses conventional frames and points of view that allow him to produce such attractive results as those in figure 79, reminiscent of an Oriental painting.

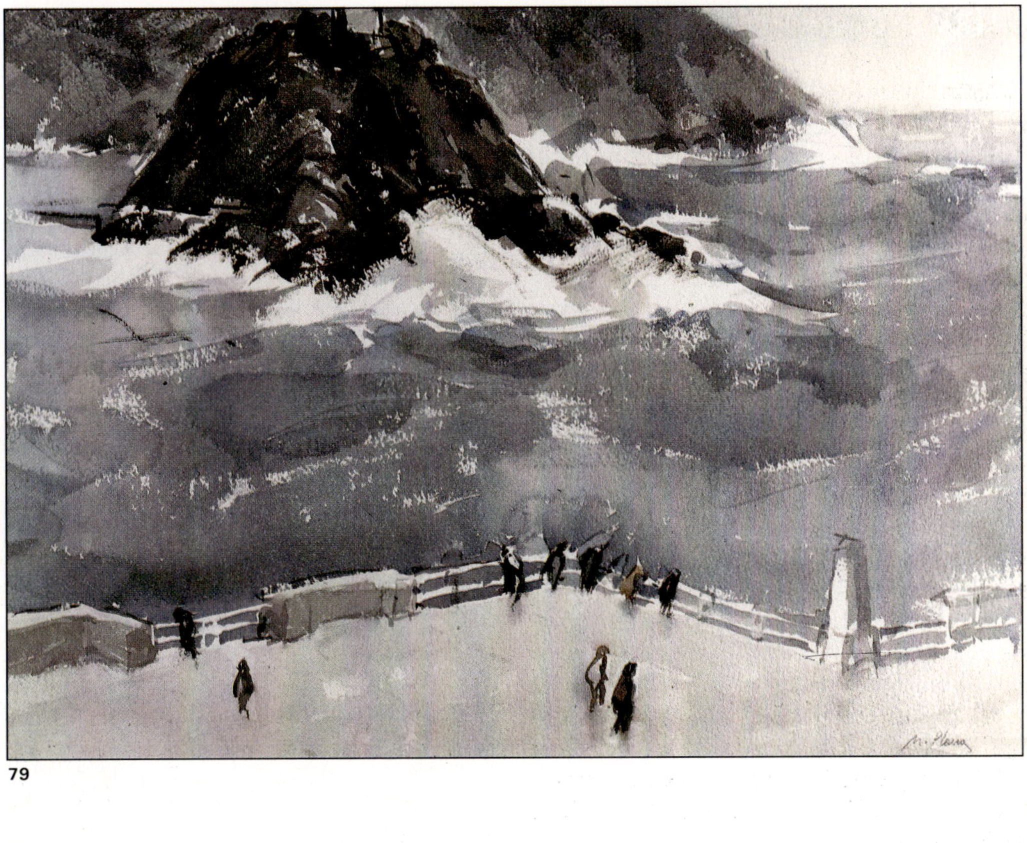

79

Drawing: a first approach to the theme

80

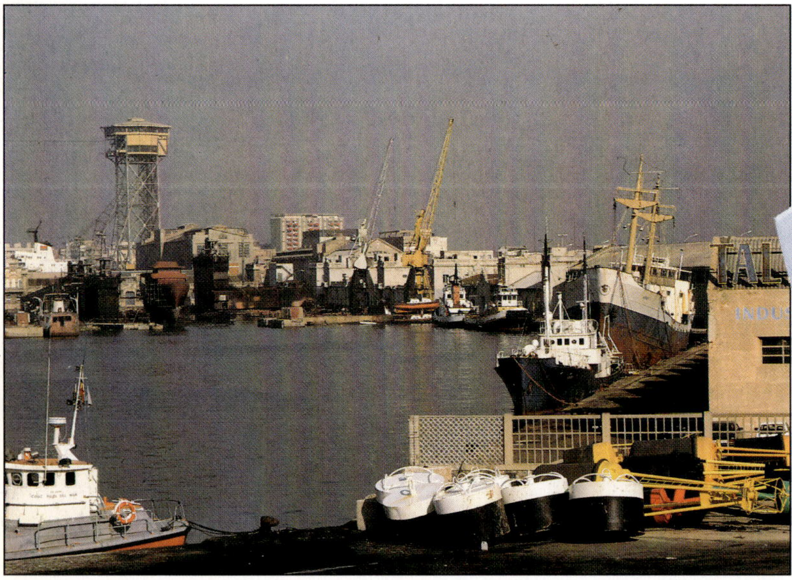

81

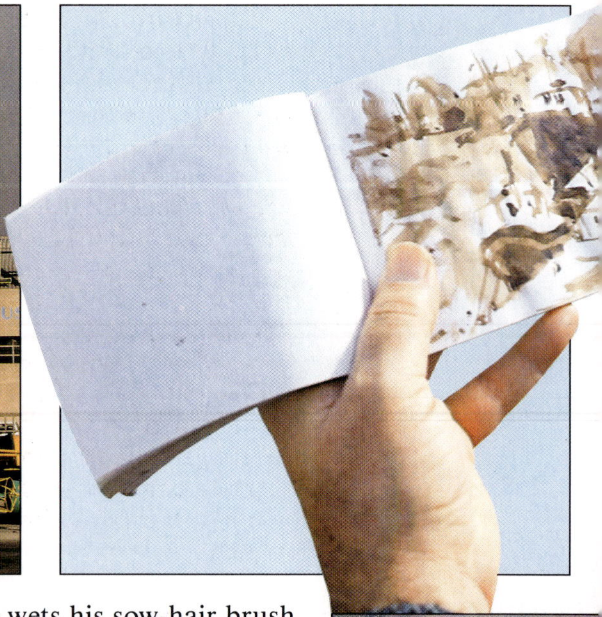

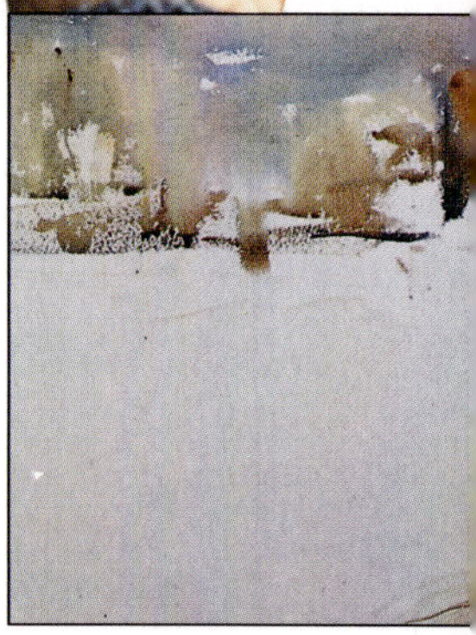

We are at the port of Barcelona, where we have come to paint a seascape. Manel Plana has made a painstaking search for his subject. In fact, he tells us, he took a walk around here a few days ago to prepare for this session. The proof of this is in the sketches he shows us, in which he has studied different possibilites. Painting out-of-doors, you cannot always have full control over your subject, for it is constantly escaping—there are changes in light or the disappearance of a particular element. That is why it is important to have a precise idea of what you want to paint.

Plana has finally opted for a theme that is already familiar to him. It is the view of the port from the breakwater seen in figure 80. There are various docks on the horizon, occupied by buildings, cranes, and towers. The horizon is blurred by the distance and by the intermittent light of this hazy, windless day. The weather conditions give a grayish, ''atmospheric'' look to the subject—typical qualities of a watercolor painting. The composition of the picture is dominated by the diagonal line of the dock on the right-hand side, with two boats, the building, and the fence in the foreground. The rest of the picture is taken up by the large central space formed by the sea.

Manel Plana mounts his paper with drawing pins. Then, he wets his sow-hair brush with sepia, which he has watered down greatly. He begins to draw, attentive both to the subject and to his sketch. At this point, he concentrates on the values and the general composition, as seen in the sketch in figure 81.

This is the sketching, study phase. Plana holds his brush at the end of the handle and lets it hang in the air a while before painting. His first lines define the main lines of the composition—a few touches on the horizon and then emphasis is placed on the diagonal. In this way, the composition forms around the empty space in the center.

Little by little, this abstract pattern of lines takes the shape of a figurative representation, as the boats, the dock, the building, and the fence are defined. He continues painting with dark lines to bring out the contrast, which is a main characteristic in the work of Manel Plana.

Next, he paints the sky, not as a uniformly colored strip, but with a variety of grays, both warm and cool, obtained from a mixture of ultramarine blue, yellow, and sienna.

The drawing is not a faithful representation of the actual subject. For example, he has altered the shape and position of the two boats in the foreground.

Fig. 80. After walking around the port, Manel Plana has chosen this view as the theme for his watercolor. In the composition, the central form—in the shape of an inverted C, consisting of the horizon and the docks—stands out.

Fig. 81. Manel Plana generally uses a small sketchbook to note the way in which he intends to approach his painting.

Step one: the background

"A picture, rather than a war-horse, a female nude or a passing scene, is above all a flat surface covered by colors related in a certain order." This statement, made around 1890 by the French painter and writer Maurice Denis, is wholly born out by the way Manel Plana sees the art of painting. "Painting," he says, "is a process of observation and interpretation where what is really important is what happens on the paper." Plana made this comment while cleaning his palette with a sponge.

"From now on," he continues, "I'll paint more quickly, and we'll have to wait and see if I get it right or not." The artist is referring to the rapid work that painting in watercolor, a technique based on wetness, demands.

Manel Plana paints over the base color of the sky, which is still wet, with yellow and blue, allowing the color stains to mix and spread. Due to the roughness of the paper, caused by the grain, these brushstrokes leave a few whites, which you can see in figure 82. He continues with his work of defining lights and shades, using his two filbert brushes alternately. With dark sienna tones, he paints in some of the buildings (fig. 83); then, with strokes of yellow paint that become diluted by the surrounding colors, the cranes appear (fig. 84). Plana paints from left to right, creating new forms and new stains. In his words, he "fills the space" with a fascinating variety of techniques that suggest the feeling of the blurred distance of the horizon perfectly (fig. 85).

82

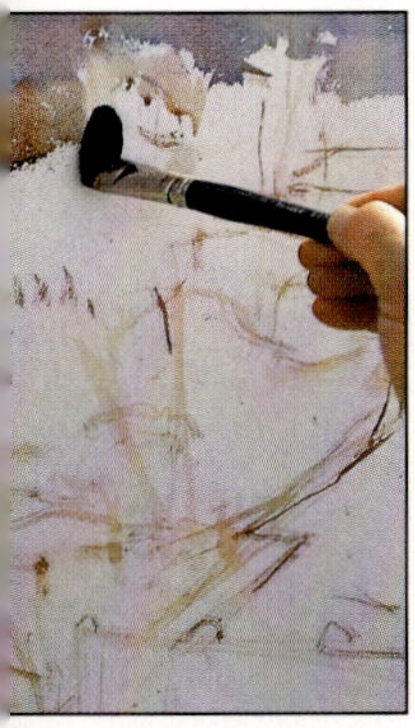

83

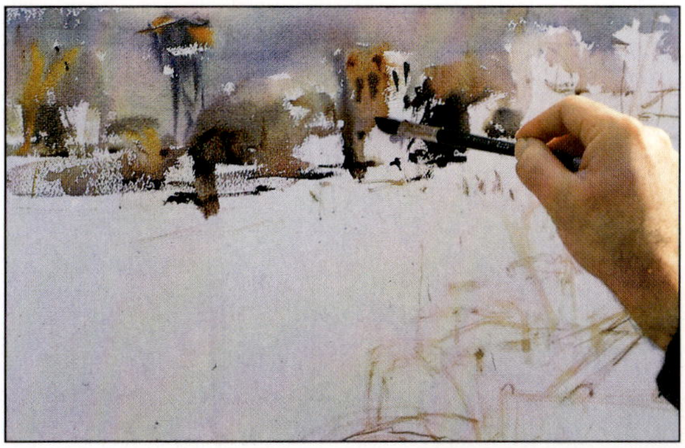

84

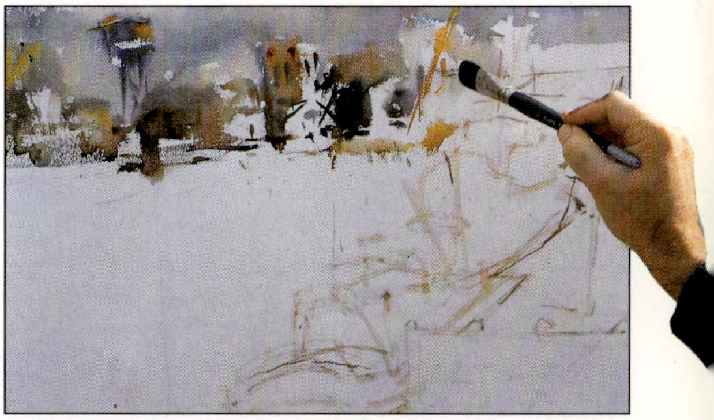

85

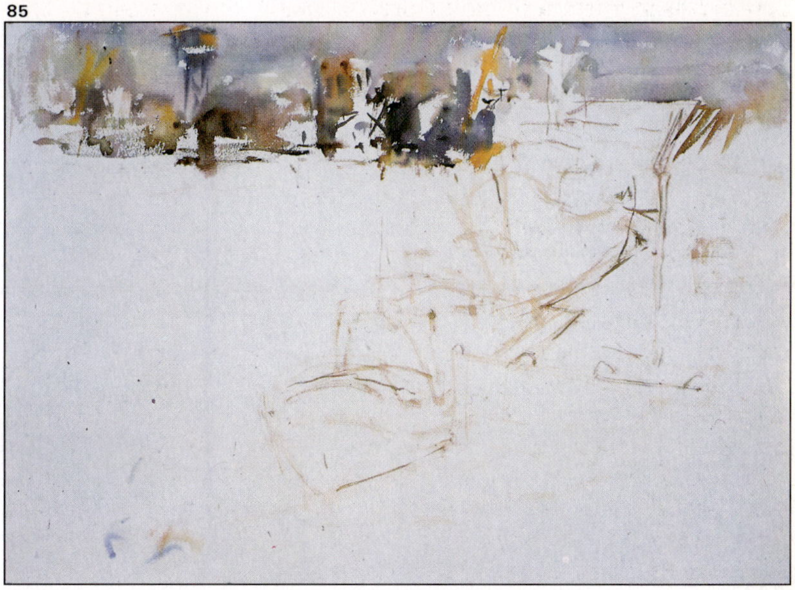

Fig. 82. After completing the first approach to his theme through drawing, eliminating some elements and adding others, the artist begins to paint the sky and the horizon.

Fig. 83. Once he has stained the area with an irregular pattern, using a light wash of blue and umber, he constructs a number of buildings with delicate, precise brushstrokes.

Fig. 84. Some of the elements in the background, such as the cranes, allow him to use purer colors. This orange, for example, enlivens the horizon.

Fig. 85. He has only been painting for a short while, and the background of the watercolor has already been defined. This combination of fast work and splendid results will remain a constant throughout the session.

Step two: a synthesis of light and shade

Plana usually begins with the background and then paints the foreground. He paints whole areas from start to finish before going on to the next area. For each area, he cleans his palette, as he does now.

With a mixture of sienna, yellow, and a little orange, he obtains a warm, earthy tone with which to work on the shadows of the horizon. He takes up a fine brush to reinforce an outline and then adds blue to paint in details. These fine strokes are applied around the middle ground of his picture, where Plana is preparing to add new colors. Manel Plana has taken his gaze from his sketch and is seeking inspiration from the live subject matter, which always offers greater richness of tones. He now studies the subject intently.

He pauses after each brushstroke, stepping back to examine the results of his work, trying not to lose his overall vision, and seeking solutions to the demands of the picture. A constant "dialogue" takes place that helps Plana resolve problems with amazing speed.

Now, with a gray-blue tone, he paints the shadow of the cabin of the most distant boat (in the middle ground) with just two stains (fig. 86). He leaves white areas which will be light zones, creating contrast through the feeling of volume, of mass. This is a precise exercise in synthesis which, of course, does not end here.

With a couple of strokes of blue, broad and fairly thick with paint, he paints the hull of the boat. He makes sure that his brush with blue stain, now mixed with a little sienna, does not spread (fig. 87). Then, with the brush even more heavily loaded with paint, he builds up the volume with great skill. There are just four stains, but they are impeccably placed on the paper.

Really, Plana working is quite a sight to see. It is difficult to describe each action. Sometimes he moves closer and then farther away from his painting. As he works, Plana squeezes his brushes between his fingers to clean them or to get rid of excess water. Sometimes, he shakes the brush vigorously so that the ground around him is dotted with drops of paint.

86

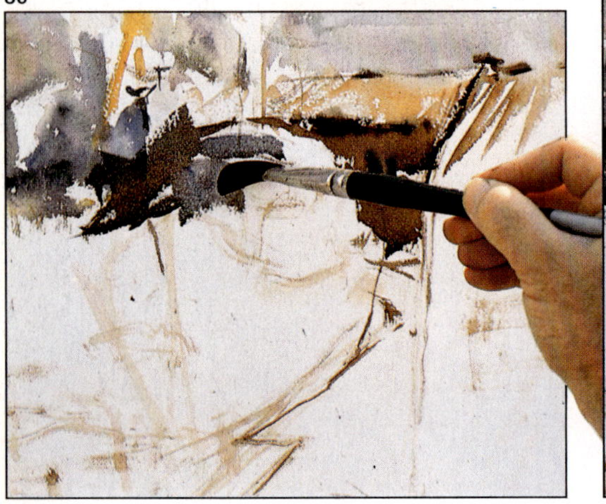

87

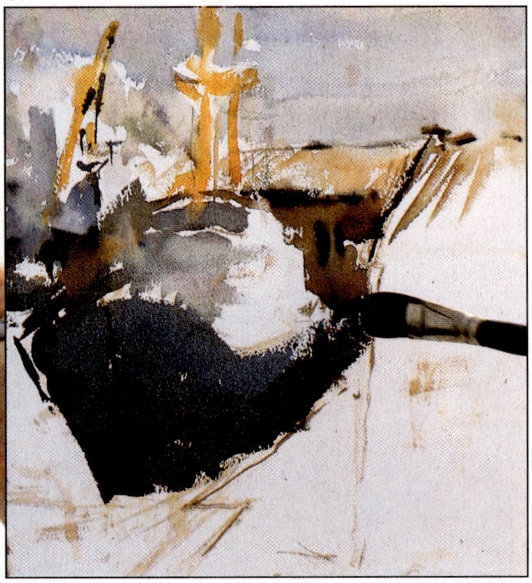

Fig. 86. To express, to paint, with the minimum of possible resources, that is the key factor of this watercolor. Manel Plana begins to paint the ship's cabin; he uses the white of the paper to represent the strongest light section.

Fig. 87. Here the artist gives shape to the objects in his picture through the definition of zones of light and shade, using this technique first with the cabin and then with the hull of the ship. Two brushstrokes of deep blue are sufficient to define volume.

88

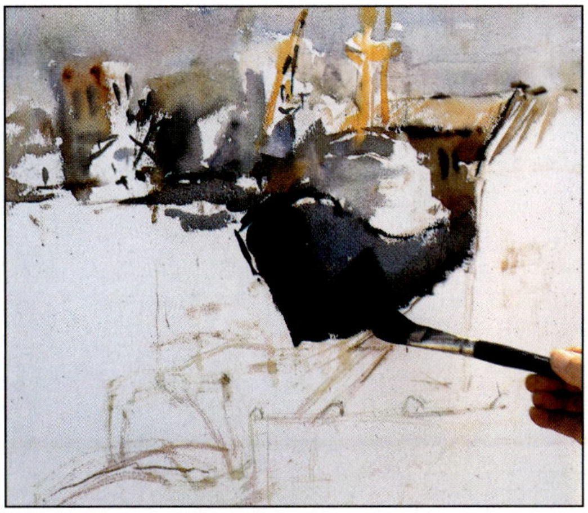

But let us get back to the paper. Once the areas of light and shade that make up the boat have been situated, our guest artist paints in various details, just enough to bring out the overall effect. Then, he scratches the paint and produces a clear line that forms a shine on the prow of the steel hull of the boat, strengthening the contrast between the colors in the shade.

With orange, he paints the aerials of the boat, letting these three lines blend in with the background. A few little touches of ultramarine blue complete the features of the vessel (fig. 89).

This stage of work has given us the opportunity to witness a splendid session of fresh, free, direct painting. Plana is the kind of painter who has an enormous sensitivity to the different effects of the light, which he expresses with the greatest economy of means possible (fig. 90).

89

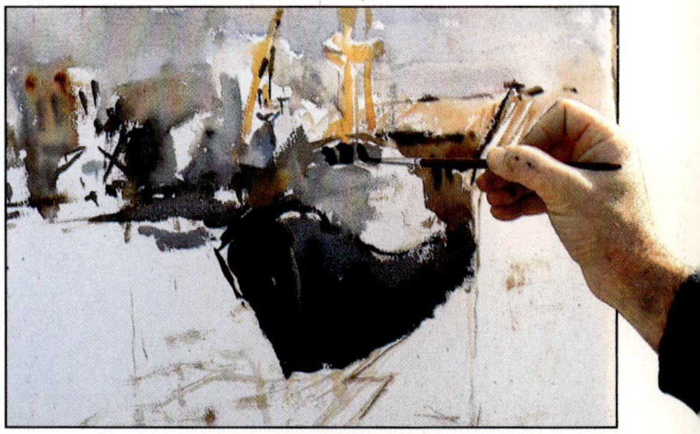

90

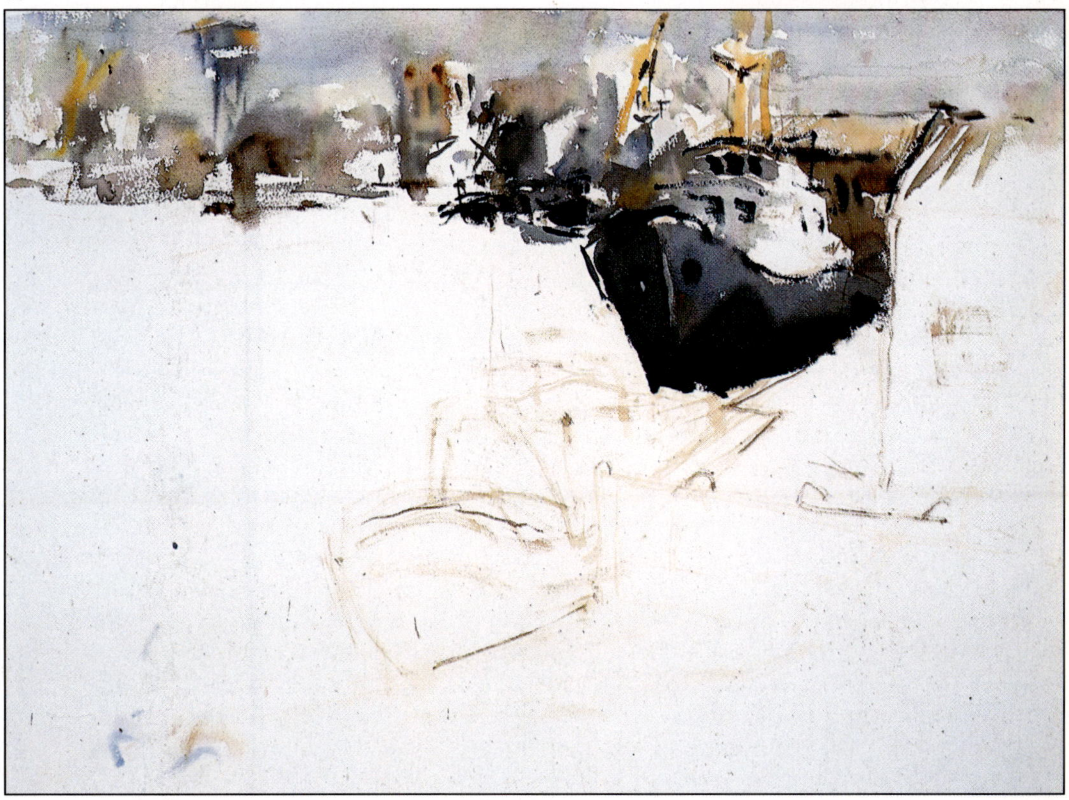

Fig. 88. With each new color he uses, Manel Plana bears in mind the surrounding tones. It is the same with the shadows; he provides color on both the object casting the shadow and the shadow itself. Here, he paints a shadow that is cast by a building on the right, which he has not yet painted. The shadow spreads over the quay, covering part of the ship's hull.

Fig. 89. Once he has established the basic relationship between light and shade in each object, Plana then gives these objects their character and features, painting in aerials, windows, shines, and so on.

Fig. 90. In a flash, Manel Plana applies the touches that give shape to the ship. Summarizing, simplifying, synthesizing continually, the artist demonstrates his technical mastery of the art of painting in watercolor.

Step three: the stain

91

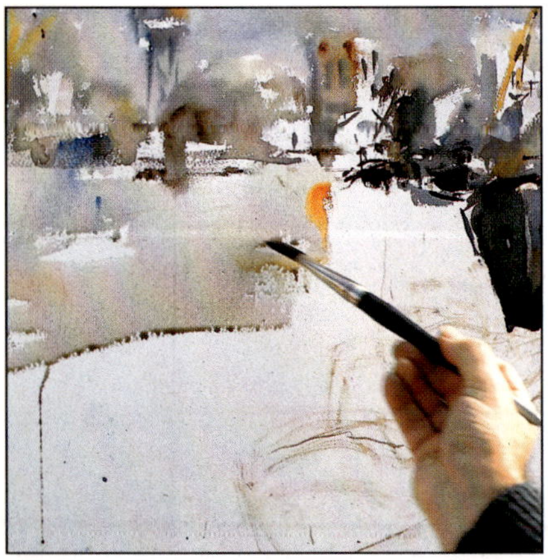

92

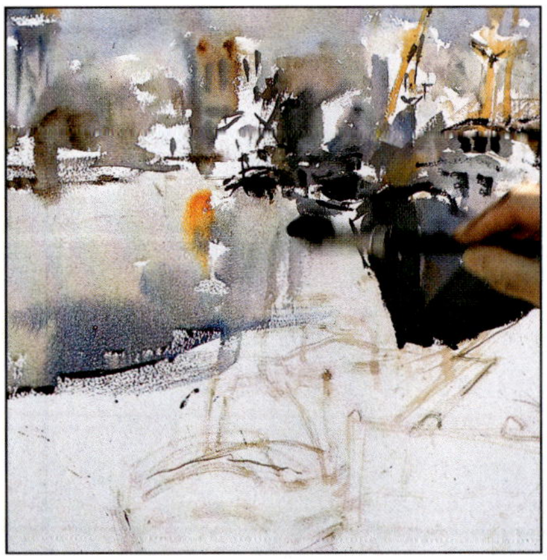

93

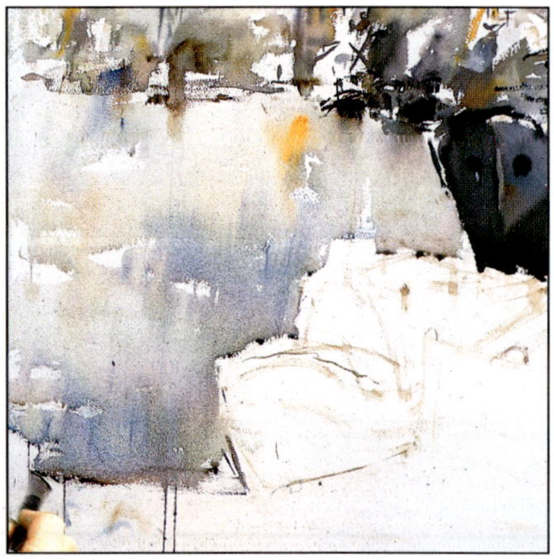

94

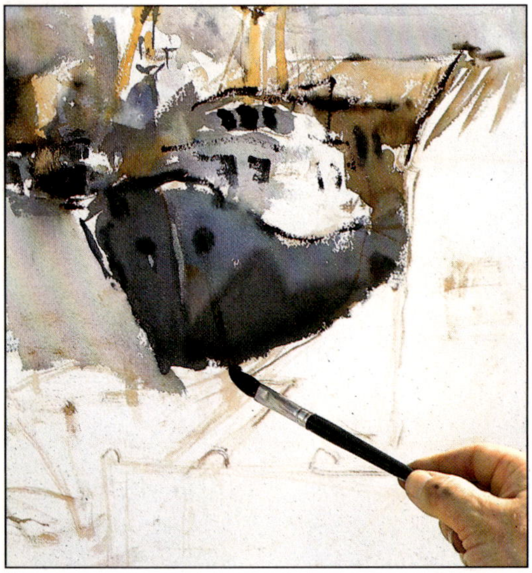

95

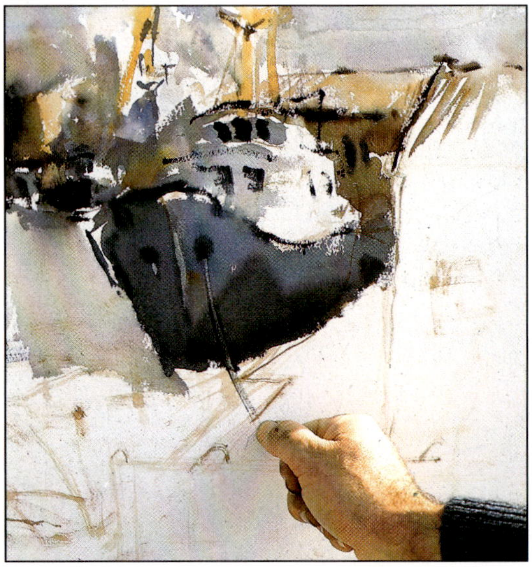

Manel Plana is about to paint the large light area in the center, which is actually the sea. He mixes a grayish tone on his palette and loads a large quantity on his brush. With the brush well laden with paint, his strokes create transparent, irregular stains (fig. 91), which Plana allows to run and mix in with other colors at random. The paint spreads over the paper from top to bottom, like a curtain slowly falling (fig. 92). The stain is not a uniform color; it is enriched by other tones, earthy colors, yellows, blues, and violets. The entire paper is not covered. Plana leaves some white areas to provide a subtle transition between the colors he is using, and to suggest, without overdoing the stains, some spontaneous-looking shiny areas on the surface of the water.

The colors of this area, though much paler, mostly echo those he has used in the background. He now returns to the shadows, adding a few more light touches.

Plana has taken great care to reserve the area to be occupied by the boat in the foreground, which at this point he has only sketched into his picture, as you can see in figure 93. Before painting this element, the artist gives us another lesson from his vast experience. Using the same technique as he has already shown us, scratching with his finger, he "moors" the boat he has painted. First, he draws a thin blue line; then he brings it out by scratching the background, which is also a dark tone (figs. 94 and 95).

Fig. 91. To paint the sea, he dips his brush in a grayish wash and paints from left to right on the paper. At times, he allows the paint to run, but never overdoing things.

Fig. 92. He also spreads the paint with this brush, using an upward movement to contrast with the previous direction. Next to the soft zones, he paints thick stains of blue or orange to emphasize the contrast between brushstrokes.

Fig. 93. Manel Plana avoids a conventional treatment of the sea. Making use of his paper, he leaves some areas white to form reflections in the soft "curtain" of warm and cool tones that run down into the foreground.

Figs. 94 and 95. Now, he works again on the ship. This time he "moors" it to the quay by first drawing a blue line (fig. 94), the rope. Then, he scratches it with his finger (fig. 95) to make it stand out more against the dark base of the same blue.

Now Manel Plana mixes a gray-blue color on his palette, darker than the color used for the sea. Using this new tone, he paints a shadow which, set against the white of the paper, defines the volume of the boat's cabin. Next, with a firm stroke of the brush that was dipped in a warm sienna tempered by a little orange, he paints the stern, the part of the boat facing us.

Here, volume is achieved with a heavy brushstroke of sienna and indigo, and another brushstroke that absorbs a strip of paint. A clear line is created that contrasts with the stain which it lies within. To finish, Plana cleans off a few unwanted drops with a sponge (fig. 96).

This boat has obviously been painted according to the needs of Plana's picture. It is not a copy from real life, as you can see if you compare the composition on this page with the photograph on page 30.

A quick look at the overall effect in figure 97 reveals that, little by little, the watercolor is acquiring a tonality somewhere between blue and sienna, between cool and warm. However, this overall tendency does not exactly follow the traditional composition of a painting, which places cool colors in the background and warm colors in the foreground. In fact, cool and warm tones are found all over the picture—in the background and in the foreground—giving unity to Plana's seascape.

96

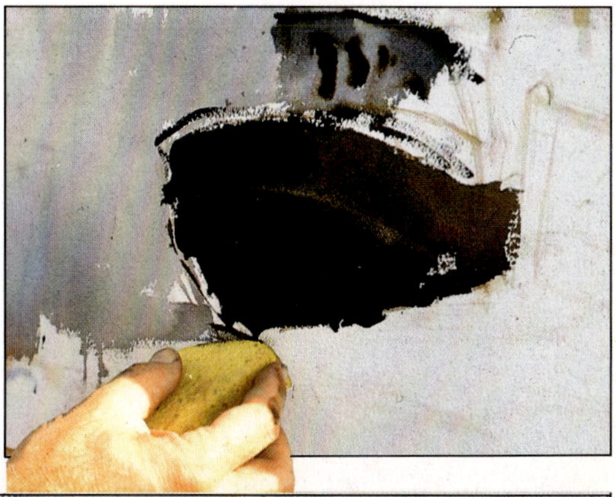

97

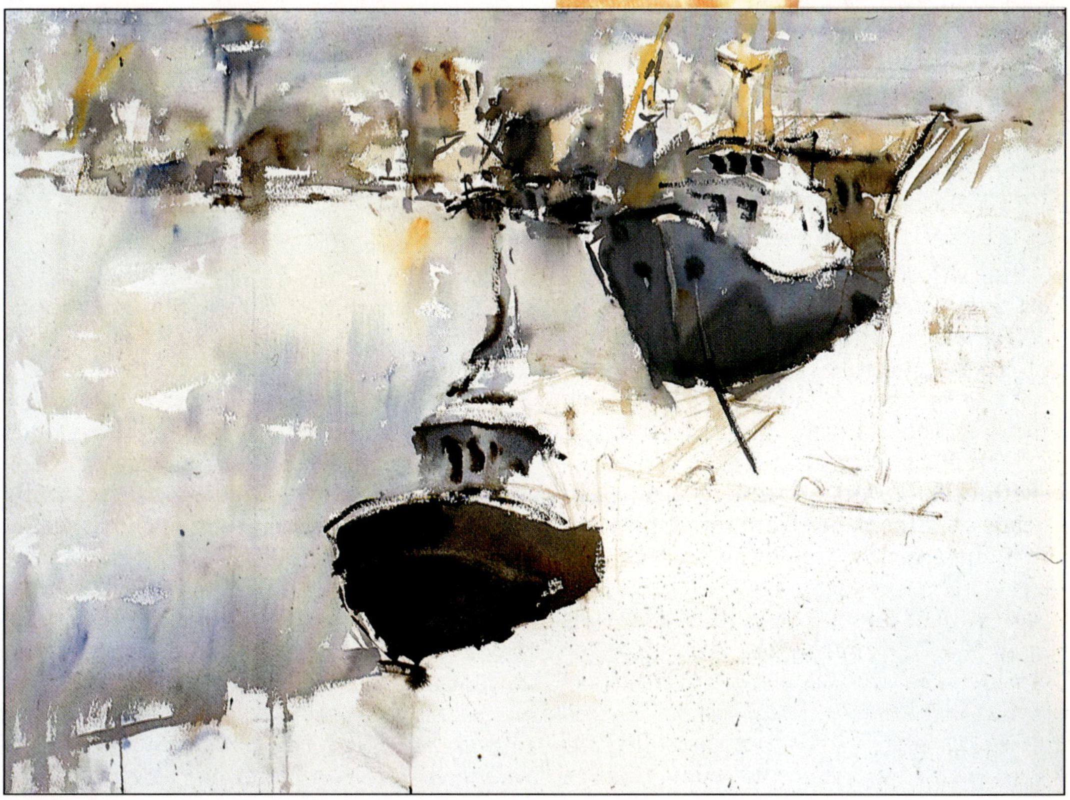

Fig. 96. When painting in watercolor with a heavily loaded brush, undesired runs frequently occur. Immediate action, cleaning with a sponge or brush, will make the effects of these accidents practically imperceptible at the end.

Fig. 97. A forceful diagonal line now divides the painting into two, separating the painted area from the one that is still white. The background and foreground have been gradually built up, from the more blurry horizon almost up to the foreground, where colors and forms are more precise and emphatic.

Step four: the foreground

98

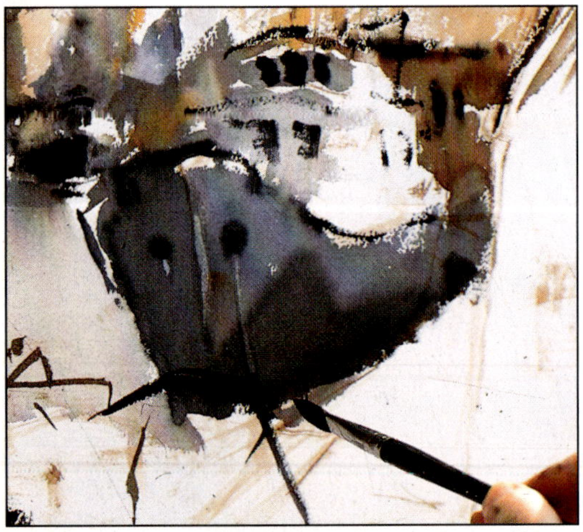

99

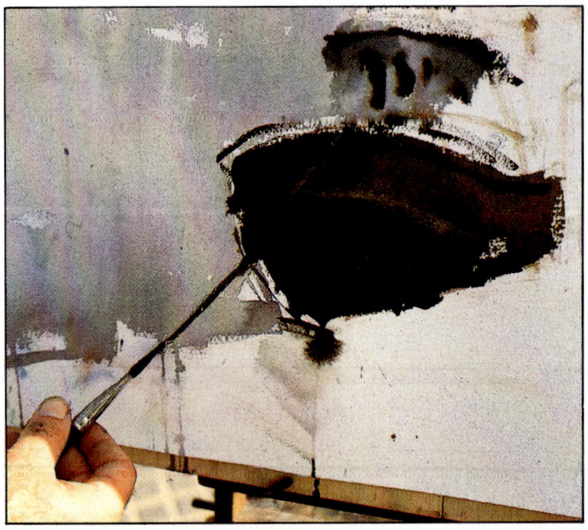

Fig. 98. Manel Plana observes the boat in the foreground and outlines its shape a bit. He attaches no importanco to the fact that the new lines are superimposed over the ship, which he has already painted.

Fig. 99. With the same method used before, Plana now "moors" the second boat. Note the simplicity with which he has painted this boat: a thick stain of broken color, a dark umber tinged with a little red, reinforced by a slightly lighter curved line.

100

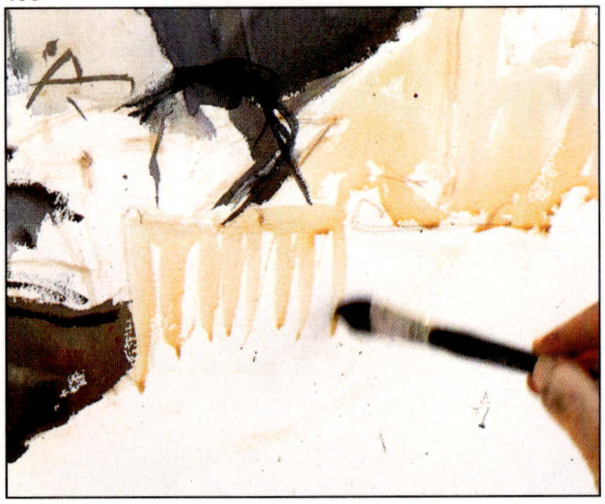

101

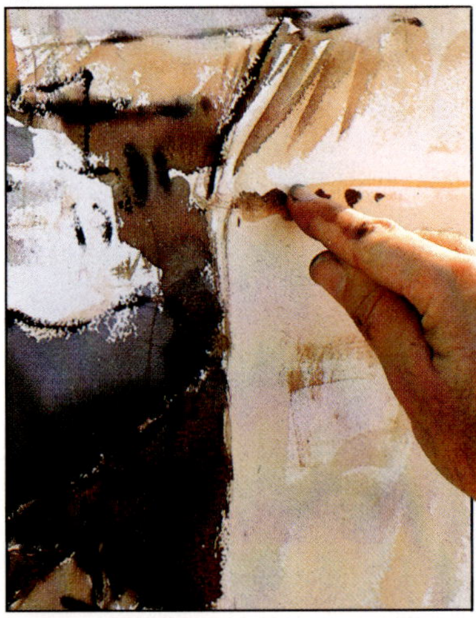

102

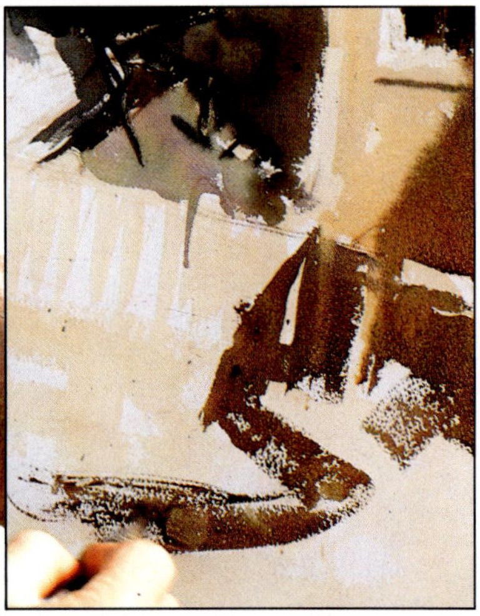

Fig. 100. Manel Plana has now begun to paint the foreground, the area in light. He covers the area with a light, very soft orange wash. For the time being, everything, the building, the fence, the ground, has the same appearance.

Fig. 101. As you have seen before, Plana is not afraid to use his fingers as a paintbrush. Sometimes he uses them to erase, and, as in the present moment, to draw.

Fig. 102. Painting in watercolor on dry paper gives interesting textures where the roughness of the support breaks up heavy brushstrokes, and lets whites show through.

The speed at which Plana has been working up to now seems to be slackening a bit at this point. At this stage of the painting, there is a forceful diagonal line that divides the composition, separating the painted area from the part that still has not been touched. Plana will now begin painting that area. But first, he has decided to complete the boat in the foreground.

With a fine brush, he paints, or "redraws." He adds several fine, graceful lines (fig. 98) that outline the prow of the boat, the windows, and the mooring rope lines, which have value in themselves because of their pictorial qualities. Here, as in other parts of the picture, the stain and the line are the key artistic elements.

With a pale orange tone, Plana now paints the foreground. First, he outlines the building with a somewhat darker line. Then, he spreads his color to the fence and to the ground. The entire section (fig. 100) is unified with this large, luminous stain that contrasts strongly with the rest of the picture. It also provides a ground that can be painted over with a darker color to achieve a transparency that is a technical "norm" of watercolor painting.

Once again he cleans his palette. "Always a good idea," he comments, as he gives the paper time to dry a little.

The elements in the foreground stand out clearly. They are well defined in contrast to the elements in the background, which have greater unity in form and tone, but are more blurred.

103

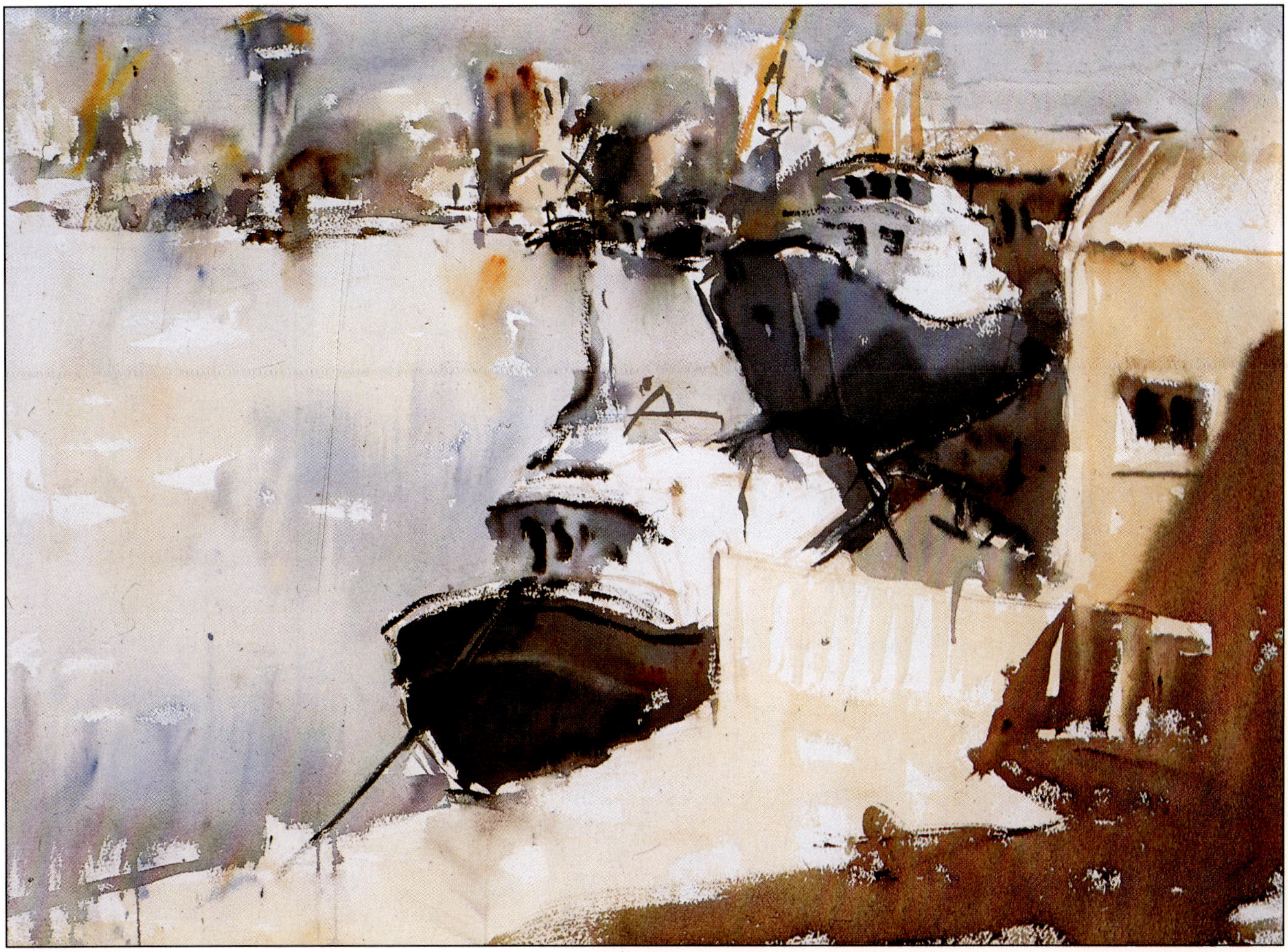

Plana will now concentrate his efforts on bringing out the "relief" effect of the foreground.

With a dark color, a mixture of indigo and sepia, he defines the area where the building casts its shadow, separating it from the background and reinforcing the feeling of volume.

The tones used to express the building's shadow are perfectly distinct from the tones on the boat and on the ground. Therefore, he blends the tones in this shadow area into a compact mass of form and color. He continues on, and, after painting in a detail or two in the building (fig. 101), he uses a clear, warm tone to paint over the light orange base of the building. By superimposing these two tones, he is able to bring out the color of the front of the building, which now becomes warmer and stronger.

He does not give the paint time to dry. Plana quickly stains this zone with broad, forceful brushstrokes, dipped in sienna. The strokes spread out parallel to the diagonal line that forms the central motive of the composition (fig. 102).

This addition exaggerates the shadow cast by the wall. He is now working on the breakwater. Once more, Plana refuses to portray the subject exactly. Instead, he prefers to supply what his picture "demands." Master of his trade, Plana reserves the space that the fence will occupy (fig. 103).

Fig. 103. Already, some changes have been made to the warm base of the foreground. To the left of the building, on the quay, there is a variation of dark tones representing the different qualities of the shadows.

The composition of the picture has been strengthened by the slant of the reddish shadow on the right, which runs parallel to the diagonal line of the quay.

Step five: completing the painting

104

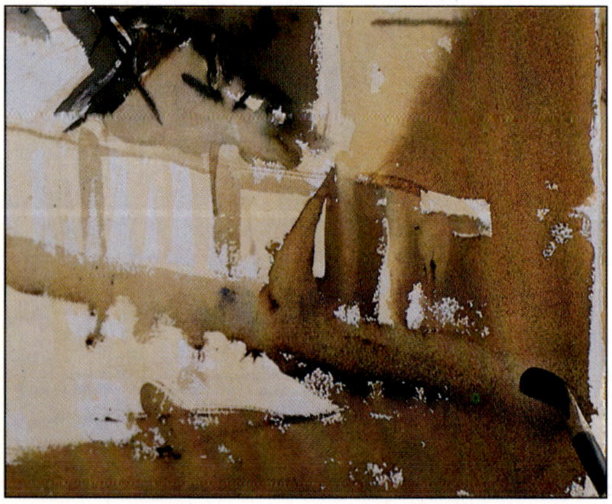

105

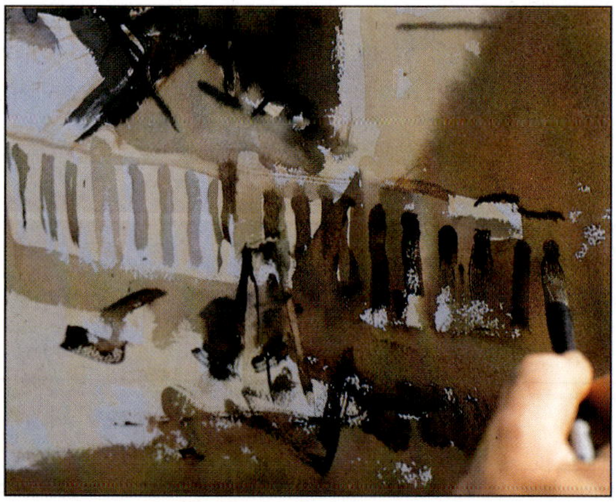

107

One after the other, Manel Plana has painted the different areas of his watercolor. He maintains the difficult balance between his own intentions and the "suggestions" made by the real life subject and the painting itself. In the end, it is this balance that will determine whether the work is a success or not. But, let us not run ahead of ourselves, Plana is still at work.

He reinforces the drawing of the fence with a number of slightly darker lines on the clear base. Using the same brush, but now absorbing the wetness of the dark base in shadow, he continues painting the fence further to the right (fig. 104). He works light on dark and vice versa, always strengthening the contrast. Then, with a bluish gray and a little yellow, he covers the ground in the foreground. Next, he uses the same tone to paint the section of the fence in the light. He paints the shadow with a few strokes of sienna as well as the bars of the fence, which you can appreciate in figure 105.

These are obviously simple techniques, but they have been acquired over years of work and experience.

Once the fence has been painted, the diagonal line of the composition is broken up and a horizontal counterpoint is created in the foreground, directly related to the line of the horizon. The structure of the watercolor has now been clearly defined into three grounds; they are unified by the dominant earthy and blue tone that covers most of the picture. The painting is almost finished. Plana now puts in the finishing touches—strokes and details placed here and there to reinforce the overall effect.

We have come to the end of the work. Plana signs his name on the right-hand side of the picture (fig. 106). "Here, filling up this space. The signature is important," he says.

An unhurried look at the picture reveals its obvious virtues. Plana has worked with an enviable economy of means. With just a few colors, he was able to create a wide variety of tones. Two strong lines, the horizontal and diagonal lines, emphasize the force and direction of the composition.

He has also taken full advantage of the possibilities that the transparent quality of watercolor offers, as well as using the white of the paper to simplify and synthesize the balance of light and shadow.

The final result, reproduced in figure 107, is a painting produced by stains, lines, and various forms and colors that exemplify the use of watercolor.

106

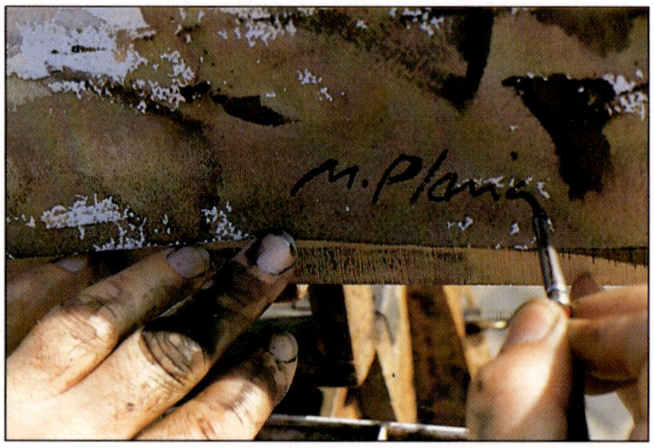

Fig. 104. Here is one method for "opening" whites on a dark background—use the brush to absorb some of the paint.

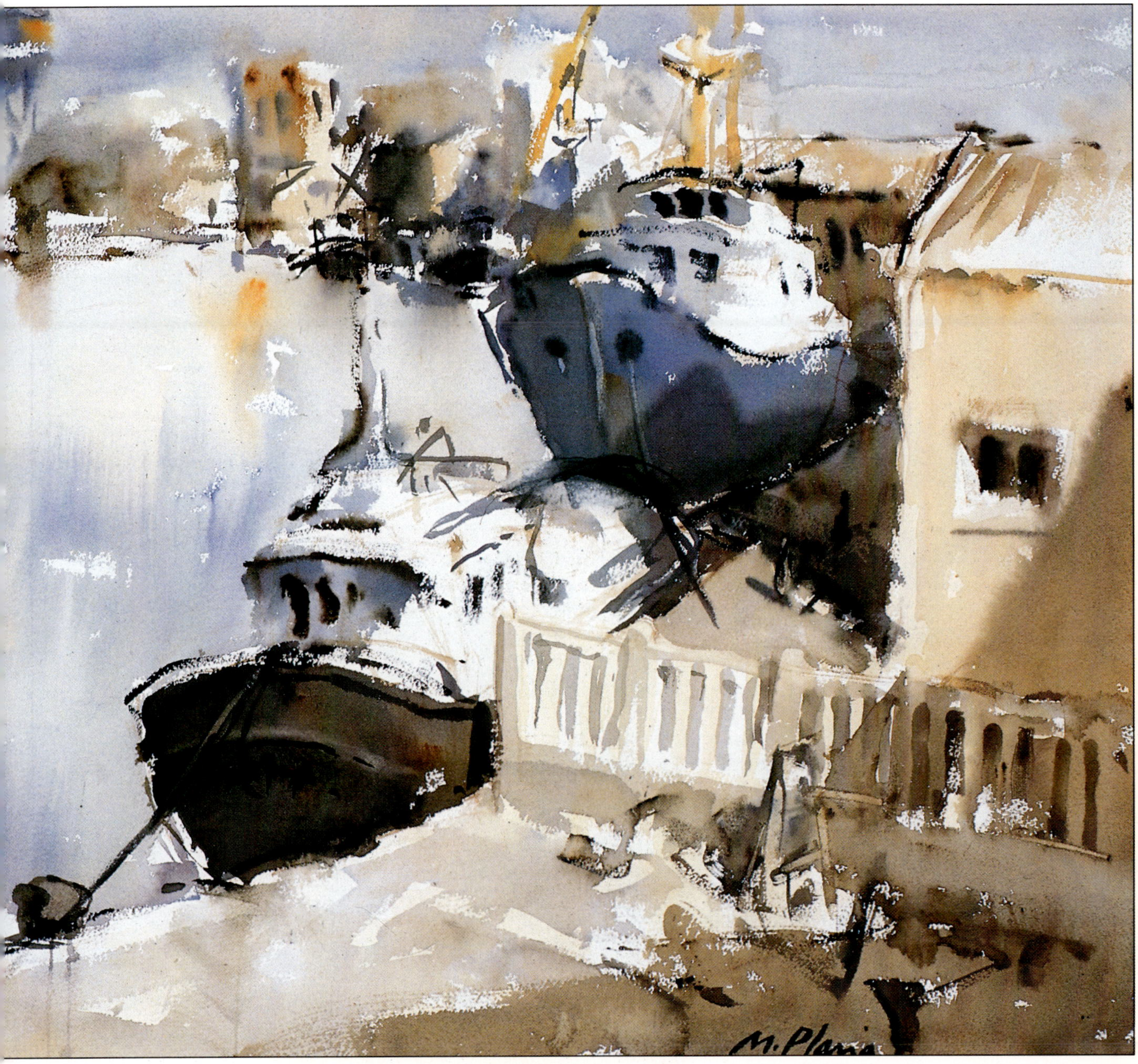

Fig. 105. By combining light and dark tones, Plana is able to suggest the transitions between light and shade that give shape to the objects in the picture. Notice the way the fence has been constructed, with bars of vertical brushstrokes of light and dark tones that create a contrast.

Fig. 106. The signature is not a secondary or unimportant element in a painting. Besides giving proof of authorship, it can be of use in the composition. It must be appropriately situated, never placed in too striking a position.

Fig. 107. This is the finished watercolor. The diagonal line of the composition has finally been balanced by the pattern of horizontal lines between the horizon and the fence in the foreground on the right.

This fence, standing out as it does, has allowed Plana to establish a series of planes that give a greater sense of space to his picture. It is also emphasized with color—warm in the foreground, cooler in the distance. Manel Plana has signed this watercolor twice—once with his name and the second time in the form of a small easel to show the presence of a painter.

Painting and artists

108

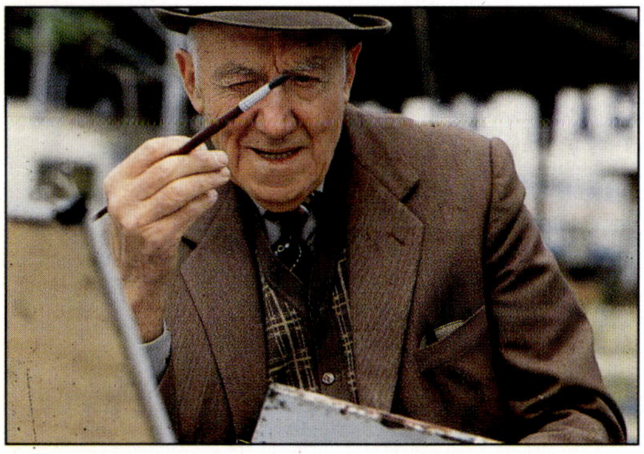

"Turner, apparently, painted fourteen-thousand watercolors. I'm getting close to thirteen-thousand." Ceferino Olivé, a painter born in Reus, Spain, in 1907, is one of the best known and most respected watercolor painters in the world, and at the age of eighty he is still painting.

There are works by Olivé in New York and Moscow. He has won the national watercolor prize and the first medal at the international salon in London, but what is most important for this painter is that he is still painting. He has created his own school, and has entered into a debate between traditional figurative painting and abstract art, in which he is in defense of the former. Soon, he will open a new exhibition.

This does not prevent him from coming with us to paint a watercolor, a seascape, twenty-four miles from Barcelona, the city where he lives. "As I don't drive, I always have to be taken everywhere, by my wife, my son, or a friend."

While we drive toward the coastal spot Olivé has chosen, we talk about paper.

Paper

Olivé, whose only son is also a professional painter, states that he does not like working with blocks of paper. He paints with precut paper or rolls, which he cuts himself. Whichever he uses, he always keeps to the classical sizes: 8, 12, 15, or 20. "The format depends on the subject, though the one I most use is 15. It doesn't matter if I'm painting figure, seascape, or landscape."

It is a cold day in May, cloudy at times. He gets to the spot he has chosen and sees a young man there mending fishing nets. He asks him if the minds his painting there. "No," is the fisherman's short but friendly reply.

The artist moves one of the nets away and starts to take out his painting box, known to younger artists as "Ceferino Olivé's paint box." There is a folding chair, water, paints, a drawing board, an easel and tripod, and painting materials. The sun comes and goes. Olivé sets up his tripod and takes out his brushes, nine in all; one is a broad scraper. Most of his brushes are very thick, no. 24 or 20; the finest is a no. 8. Some are made of sable hair, others of goat hair.

109

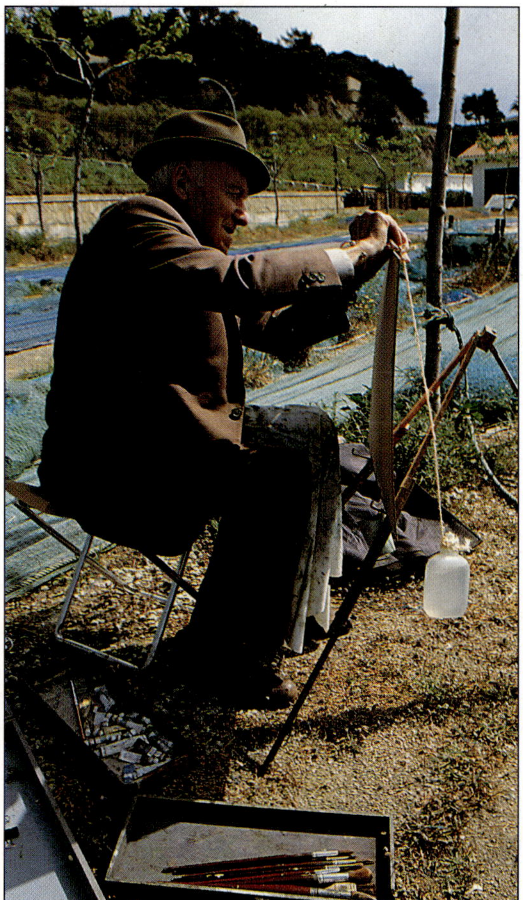

Figs. 108 and 109. This is Ceferino Olivé, a watercolor master whose work, acclaimed in Europe and America, has won him numerous prizes and awards.

The work of Ceferino Olivé

Figs. 110 to 112. Ceferino Olivé believes in a pure type of watercolor painting, without stains or reserves. His pictorial images are within the realm of traditional figurative art. Real life, therefore, is of vital importance to him, but he never forgets that it is the painter who makes the decisions. These three paintings are good examples of his extraordinary ease in painting and constructing through synthesis: The interior of the house (fig. 110) is characteristic of his somber language. He also has diversity and brilliance in his work, such as the seascape in figure 111. The third painting reproduced here (fig. 112) provides excellent evidence of the possibilities of such a demanding technique as watercolor. Olivé's drawing, composition, and color harmonization are splendid.

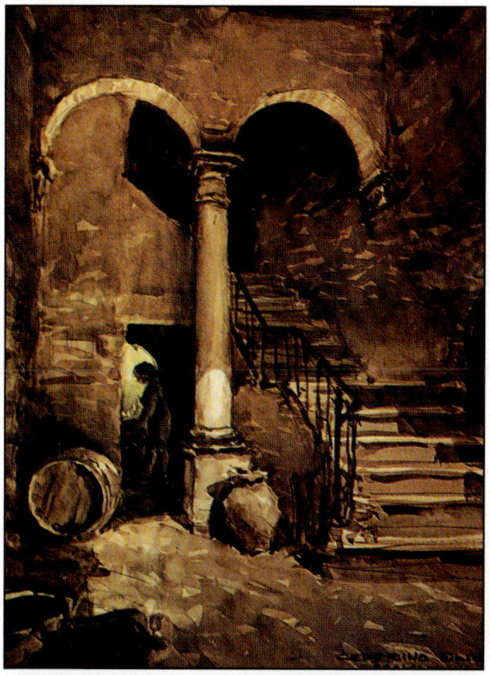

110

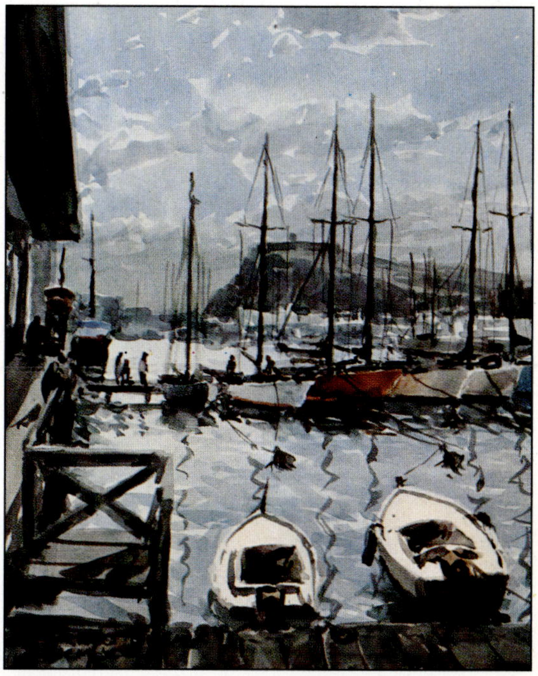

111

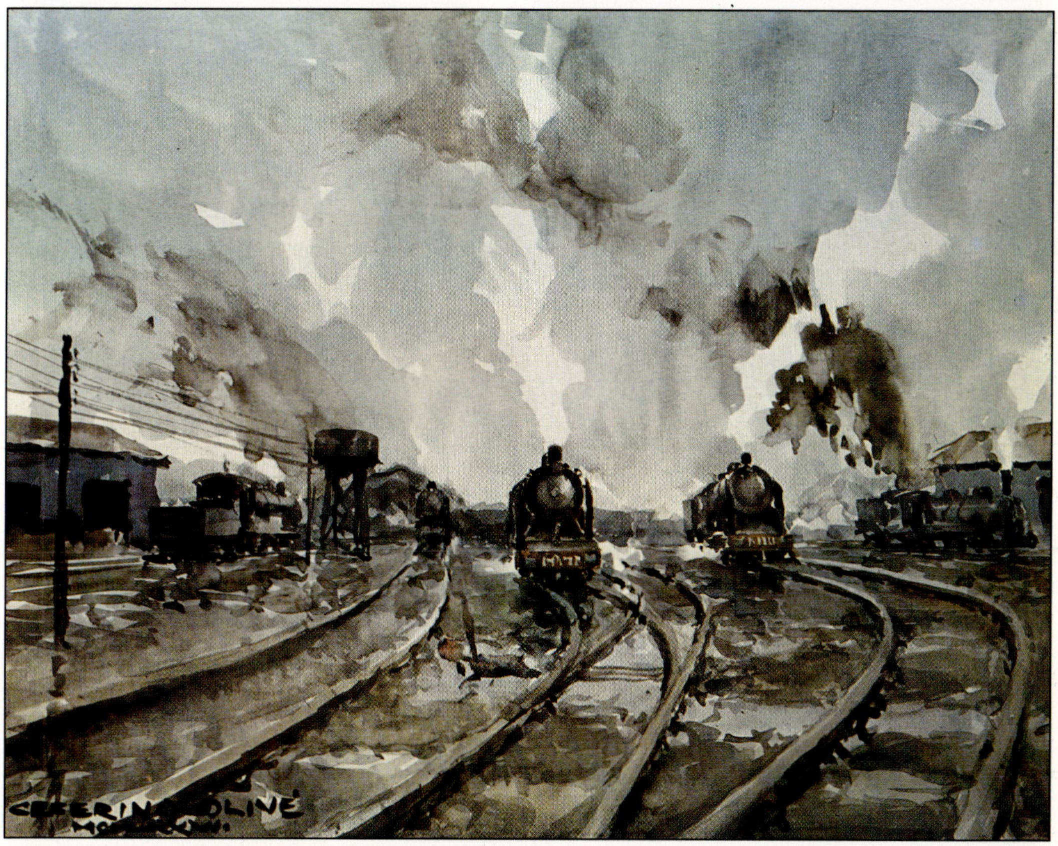

112

Step one: the sky

113

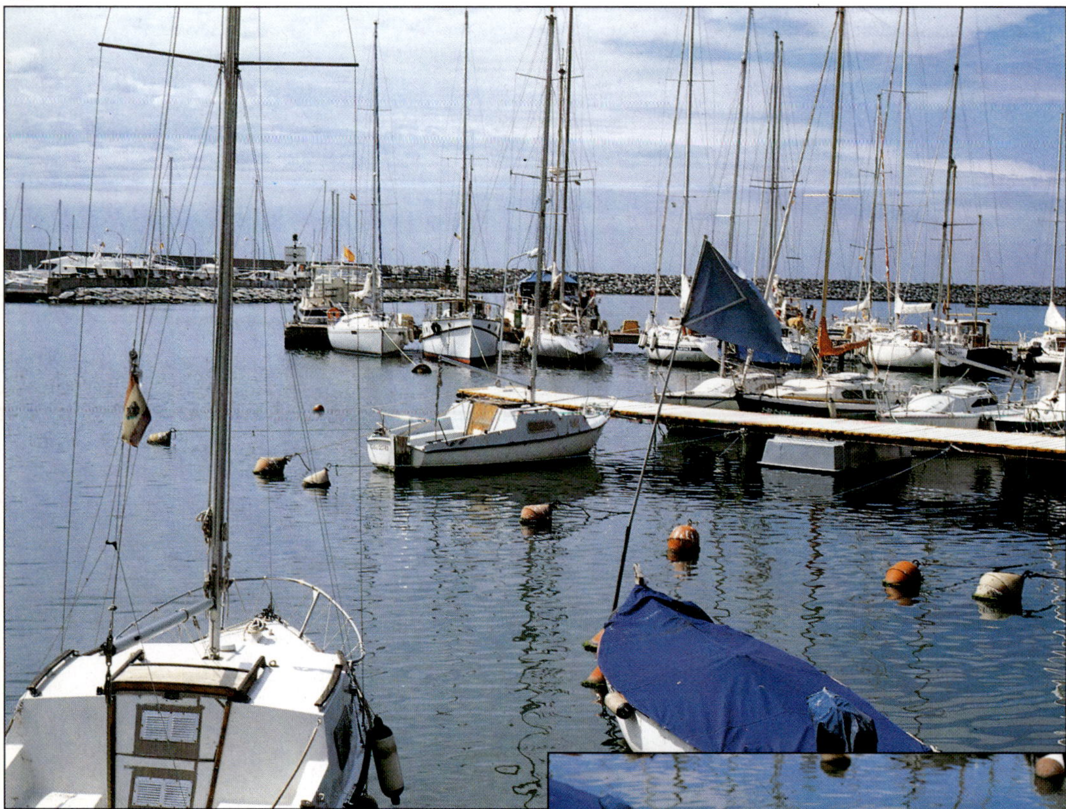

Fig. 113. The theme from the point of view that Olivé selected shows boats in the foreground, the middle ground, and the back ground. This viewpoint will help give a feeling of depth, providing what Ceferino Olivé calls "good grounds for composition."

114

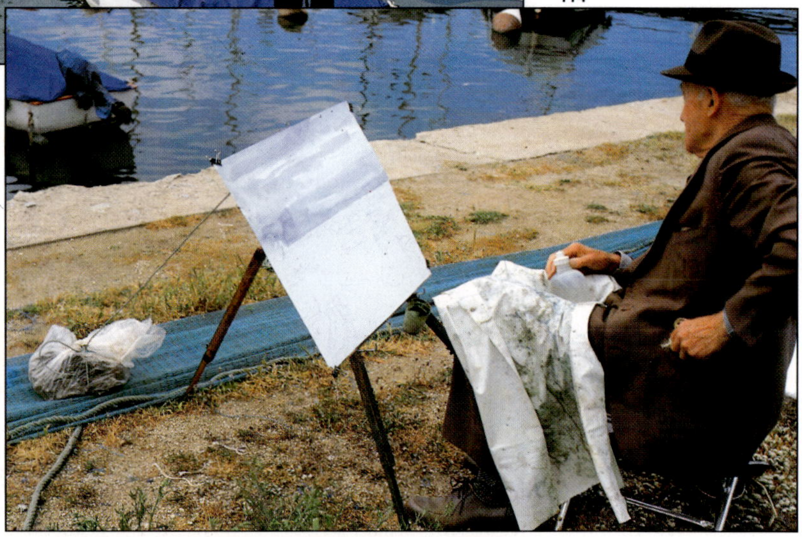

Fig. 114. Seated with his back to the light, Olivé contemplates the theme.

Olivé uses creamy watercolors in tubes made by various manufacturers. We see that he also has a couple of tubes of white gouache. As if reading our thoughts—there is an ongoing debate between watercolorists who never use gouache and those who do—he looks at us and smiles like a wise old Buddha who has long since given up any belief in dogma, and says, "It's no crime, you can use it from time to time." He goes on, "Pictures are like children. Some seem to be born with no trouble at all, others need help. Depending on which sort they are, we either let them come out in their own way or give them a hand."

He sets up the paper on this easel and begins to conceive today's child.

Choosing the position and subject

"Olivé has decided to work with backlighting—to paint against the light. It is a little after eleven o'clock in the morning and the sun is shining from the left-hand side of the subject. "At noon, the sun will be shining down right over the subject and toward the end of the session it will be a little to the right, so I'll be able to keep this backlighting throughout. If I had placed myself at a different angle, some elements that are shaded now would have come out into the sun, which would change things in my scene too much."

115

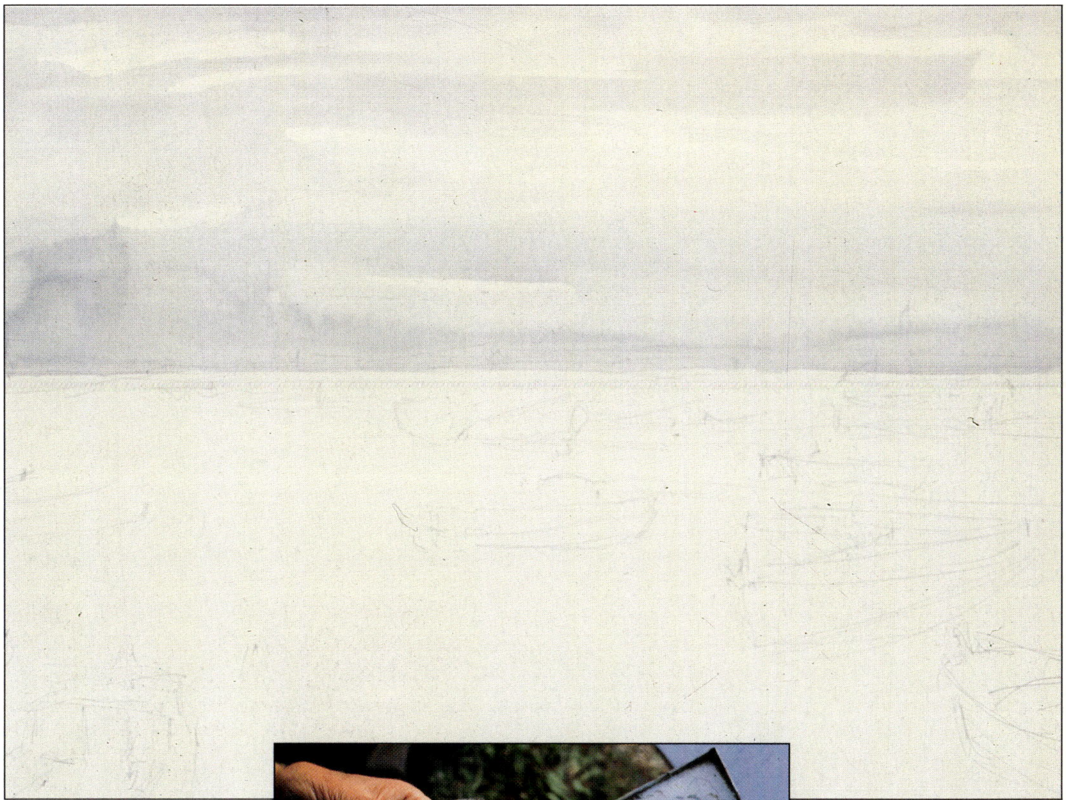

Fig. 115. The first step is to place the horizon line, to establish a relationship between the sky and the sea. The division comes close to the proportions of the "golden section." With a hard no. 1 pencil, Olivé sketches the boats, even changing the position of some of them. As the painter himself comments, "an artist can lie, I can put a boat in where I like."

Having finished drawing, he begins to paint the sky.

The weather is worsening by the minute; it is getting cloudier and the wind is building up force. Olivé starts to mix blues, mainly light ultramarine, and then dirties the mixture right away with carmine to give it more of a violet tone.

He is ready. Dipping his thick no. 24 brush into the paint, he starts to stain the sky. Working with great speed and energy, his strokes are broad and decisive. From the start, he tinges the sky with different tones so that it is not the same blue throughout. The clouds are represented by the white of the paper showing through at various points.

With the sky painted to his satisfaction as quick as a flash, Olivé shakes his brush out on the ground with great force to get rid of excess water. Then, he says, "One reason why I prefer watercolor to oil is that you finish a painting at one sitting, or at least I always do. It's a type of painting that you start and finish the same day. Generally, I finish a watercolor in an hour and a half or two hours."

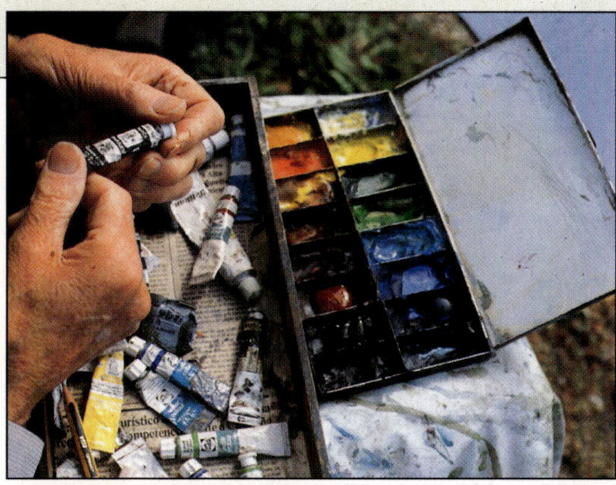

116

Fig. 116. Olivé uses creamy watercolor pigments in tubes. He has a standard palette of sixteen colors. Generally, he adds paint to the compartments of his paintbox, which usually has dried colors from previous sessions.

Ceferino Olivé's palette

All the compartments of his paintbox are full of half-dry colors. The artist puts fresh paint on top of them—sepia, burnt umber, carmine, light ultramarine blue, and light green.

Dipping his rather thick brush into water, he wets the half-dry colors. He uses the carmine compartment to mix a tone similar to burnt sienna, which he did not bring with him, and which he believes he will need.

Step two: the boats and the sea

Now Olivé takes his paintbox to mix a large amount of another color. For this new mixture, he adds blue, carmine, and sienna, and from this emerges a gray tending to a brownish mauve.

Dipping his no. 20 brush into this mixture, he sketches in the shadow of some of the boats.

He continues making more colors in the same way, from blues to greens, all with the same dirty, broken quality. With a no. 10 brush dipped into a light brown mixture, he starts to work on the boat in the foreground (a few drops of this color have run into the sea). While he washes this color out with his brush dipped in water, he tells us a little about his art.

117

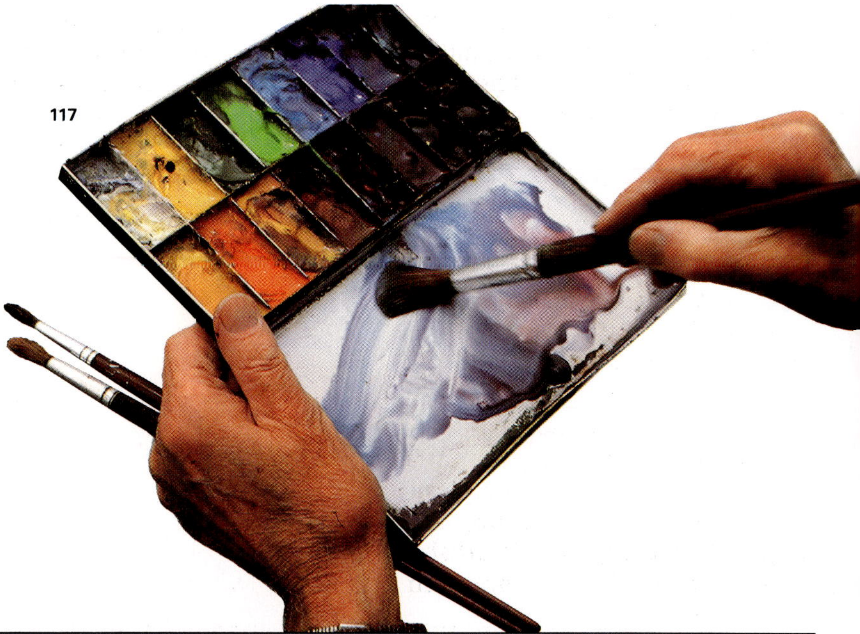

118

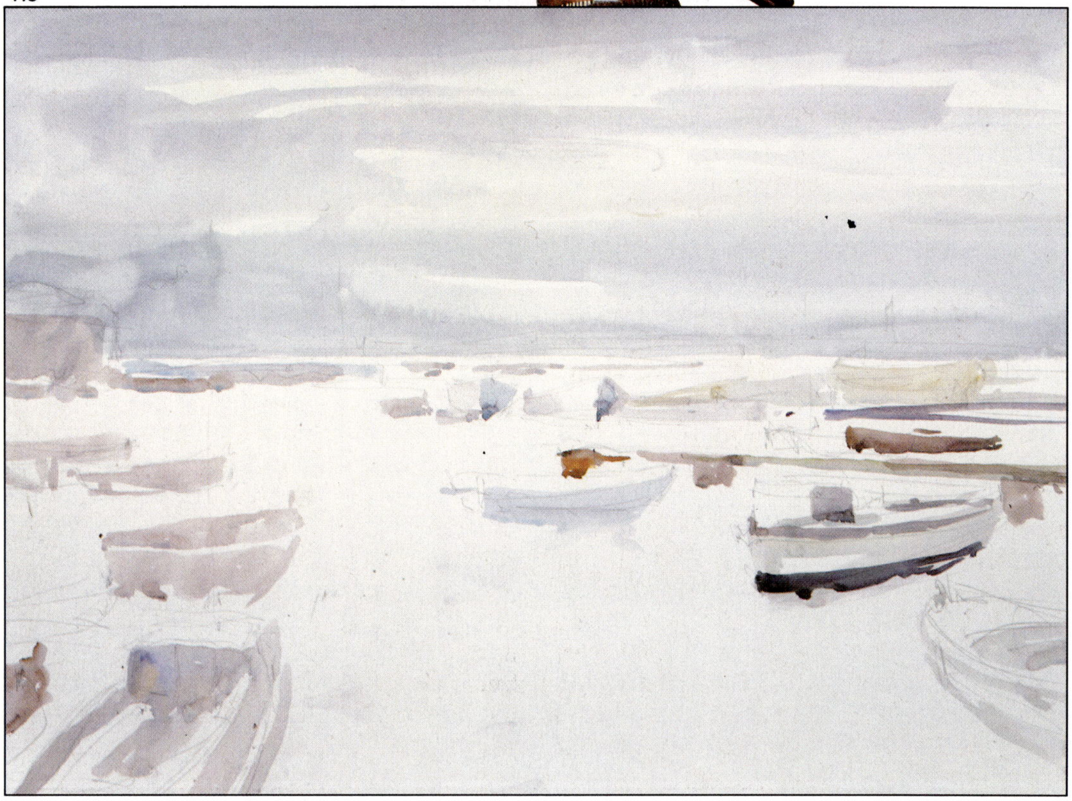

Fig. 117. Olivé takes a little ultramarine blue and carmine to obtain a violet tone on his palette. Then with definitive strokes, he paints the sky.

Fig. 118. All the areas of Olivé's watercolor painting progress at the same time. In fact, each stage could be considered as a separate painting.

"Every theme must be approached from the best side, from an aesthetic and tonal point of view. With a seascape, it's very important, regardless if you are painting with backlighting or with the sun front on. In any case, the best thing is to start with the shadows and leave the lights until later. The sun is completely covered now, but even so I'll put in a few shines at the end if they're needed."

At times, he uses a rather dark tone, a little thicker than the rest of his colors. He generally adapts his brushstrokes to the needs of each element in the picture. Some brushstrokes are very thick, while others are short strokes that outline the limits of an area with great precision.

Olivé now produces a broken blue not much different from the one he used to paint the sky, and he starts to paint the sea or the water of the port, to be more exact. First, he stains the area with sloping brushstrokes, frequently shaking out his brush to get rid of excess water. He does not stain the area uniformly, but leaves whites showing through in places to contrast faintly with this very light, dirty blue.

He now works on the line of the breakwater separating the sky from the sea. "This is a really delicate area," he tells us. Here he uses browns, mauve, and burnt sienna. He also uses these same colors to reinforce the areas in shade of some of the boats, which he had worked on earlier. With the paint, he goes over the form of some of these boats, changing them slightly.

119

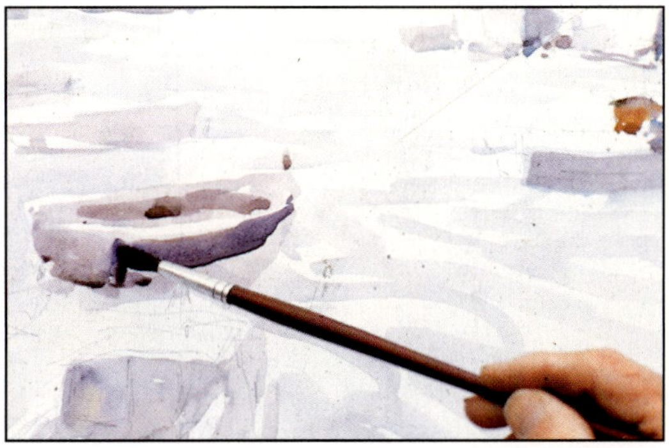

Fig. 119. Olivé holds his brush high up the handle. In this way, he is able to distance himself from the painting. It gives him a looser feel to his painting, and he can avoid excessive attention to detail.

Fig. 120. At this stage, he is well advanced in his definition of the drawing. Since the boats are constantly moving elements, they can present a problem in composition and tone. But once they are on their way to being finished, so is the overall composition of the picture. "Working with the elements provided by reality to produce an artistic creation"; this is an old formalist struggle.

120

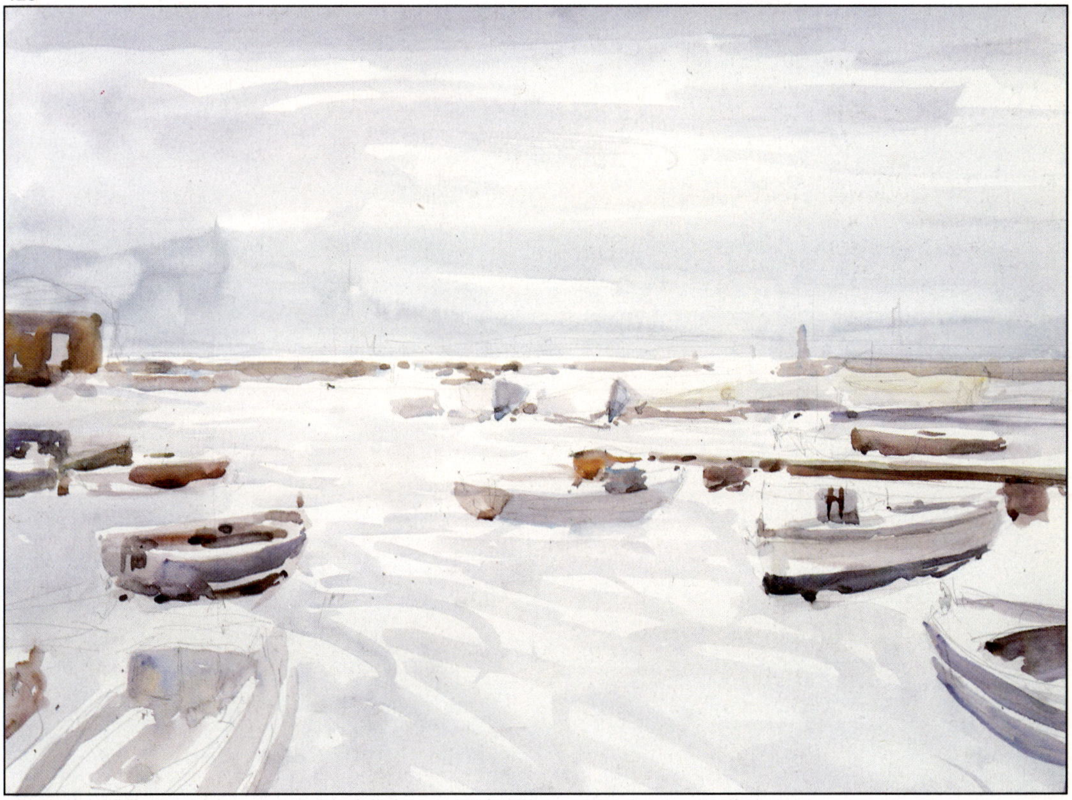

Step three: a pictorial sense

After a short pause, Olivé shows us one of the tricks of the trade, which he considers permissible. "This is no crime either," he says, with a smile as he shows us a strip of wood. Then, he proceeds to place it vertically over the picture to paint the mast of the boat on the left-hand side of the foreground. The line he makes with this ruler is perfectly straight, but he immediately goes over the line with freer brushstrokes, giving it what he calls a more pictorial quality (see figs. 121 and 122).

Having filled the left-hand side of the picture, he moves to the center. With dirty tones he paints, alternately, horizontal strokes and short stains. He continually makes new mixtures of paint, always producing broken colors. He paints the reflections in the water of the boat, which lies almost exactly in the center of his composition. If any unintentional drops of paint fall onto the picture, he immediately stumps them a little, but they do not seem to overly concern him.

Now, he goes over the hectic brushstrokes of the sea with more hectic strokes that are also darker. These strokes cover part of this area, but still leave whites showing through

Figs. 121 and 122. The decision over what is the right thing to do and what is not becomes strictly personal when painting. Some artists may not approve of the way Olivé uses a ruler here to draw the straight masts of the boats (fig. 121). But for him, this is just another resource that makes his work easier and which certainly produces fine results (fig. 122).

121

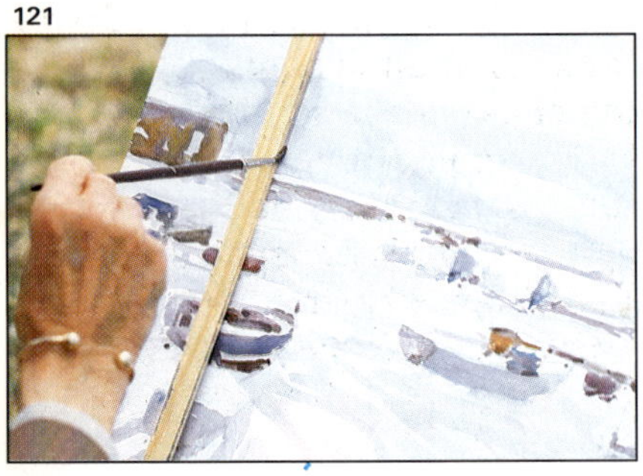

122

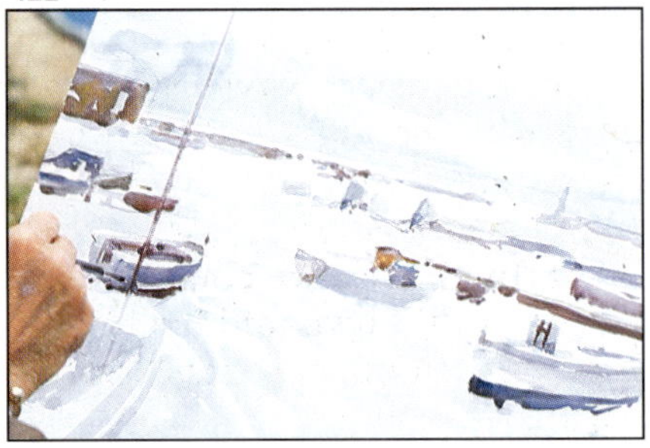

123

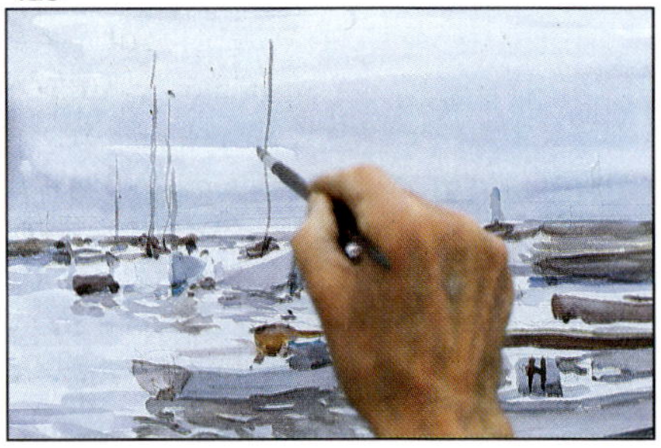

124

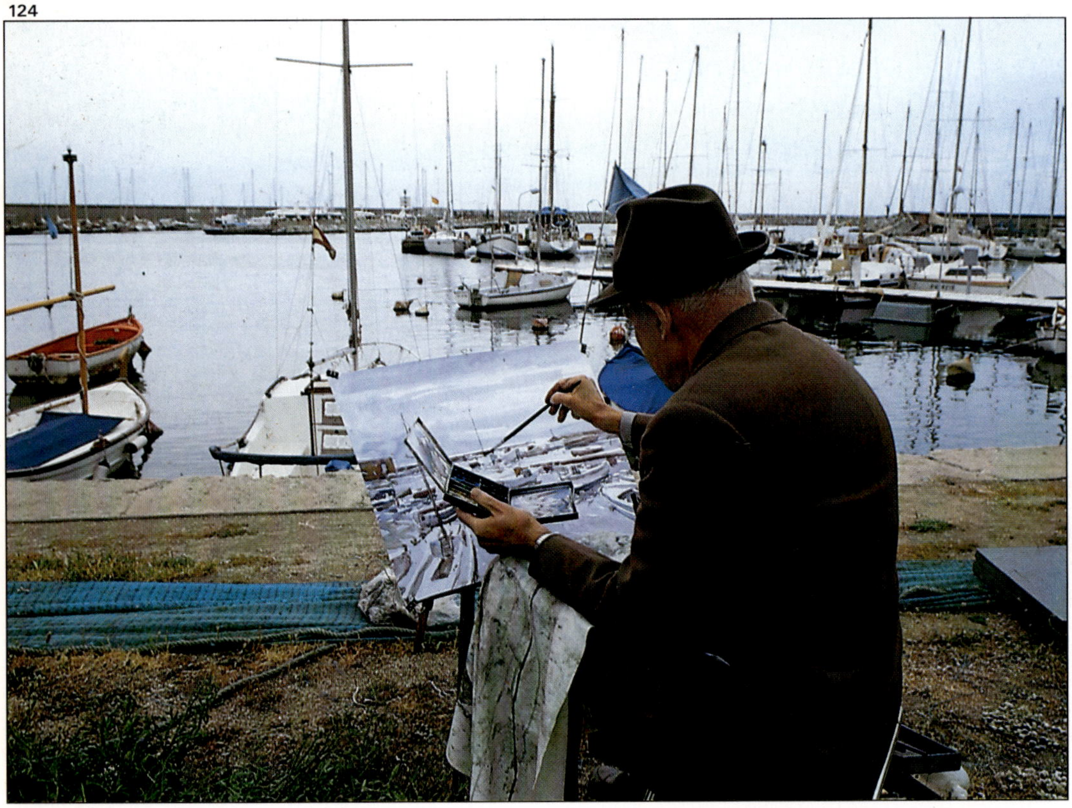

Fig. 123. The sky is the only element in the watercolor which, since it was stained, has not been altered. Olivé has merely "opened" a white or two with the wet tip of his brush.

Fig. 124. Simply but comfortably situated, Olivé continues working. Each new stain, every mark on the paper, bears the imprint of his will and character. Painting generally, but watercolor in particular, allows this gesture, this moment, to be recorded forever. This is the "pictorial style" of our guest artist.

in places, as well as some of his previous painting. This is all done in a pictorial way, as Olivé says.

What does Ceferino Olivé mean by pictorial painting? Uniting theory and practice, the artist paints with broad, loose strokes over the sea area while he answers our question. "These *hectic brushstrokes* are pictorial painting. When the watercolor is finished, it will still have an unfinished look about it, because some of these brushstrokes will still be visible." The artist's touch, the imprint of the fleeting moment, will still be there on the paper to be seen. This idea seems reminiscent of the Japanese Zen concept of art, but we are not here to debate with the artist, only to watch and record how he works and to report what he says.

Olivé pauses and says, "Oil lets the painter cover over his sins. In watercolor, the artist is naked; in fact, what we could call his nervous system, his own unique character, is transparent. In oil, few have left their mark as visibly as in a watercolor, Mir or Sorolla, for example. Although they painted in oil, their temperament shows through in their painting."

Some parts of his picture now contain a rather compact, dark watercolor. From time to time, the artist changes his brush, generally using a thicker one, but sometimes picking up a no. 10 or 12. At the end of this stage, the sky looks just as it did at the beginning, the sea now contains a number of hectic brushstrokes, and the boats have been given more of a relief effect, as you can see in figure 125.

For the time being, unless he decides to make some last-minute changes, Olivé feels that he can consider the sky finished. But the easel is in danger of being overthrown by the wind. We help him find a large stone which, wrapped in plastic and tied to his easel, will, we hope, stop this from happening. His seascape has now been anchored down.

125

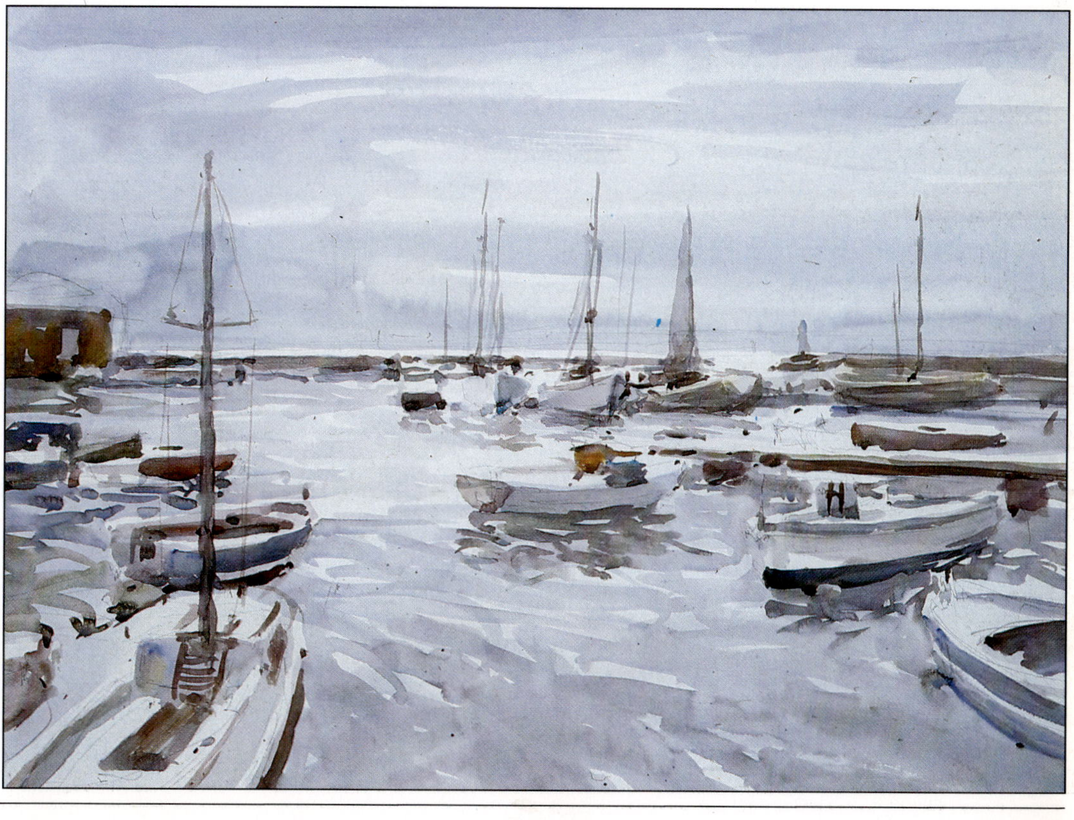

Fig. 125. The sky, the sea, and the boats ... Olivé carefully models each element with their shadow in his picture. He affirms each element with a different, new tone. The composition, with its notable horizontal tendency, has been balanced by the vertical lines of some additional masts.

Step four: adding details

Olivé outlines the vessels of his picture precisely yet with great spontaneity. Raising his head to look at his theme with rapid movements, he paints over the same area repeatedly. He is now using really dark colors. For the first time since he began painting, Olivé changes the water in his pot.

While his boats slowly but surely take on volume, Olivé tells us that he believes that Chinese and Japanese watercolor artists stifle their inspiration of the moment with formulism.

"I don't like Japanese watercolor, it's too stiff. The Japanese and the Chinese have a high-flown, very precise way of painting, but it isn't pictorial painting."

He adds a few touches to the foreground of the water, letting them run a little, just a very little. "You can sometimes let watercolor spread over your paper so that it creates its own effects, but you mustn't overdo it. Watercolor is a toy, but you can't play around with it too much."

126

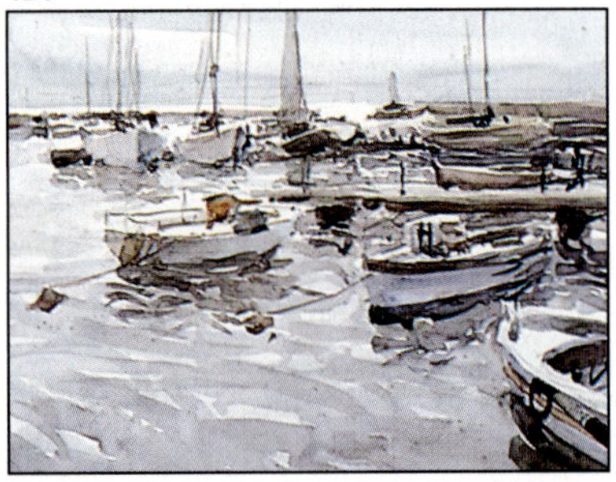

127

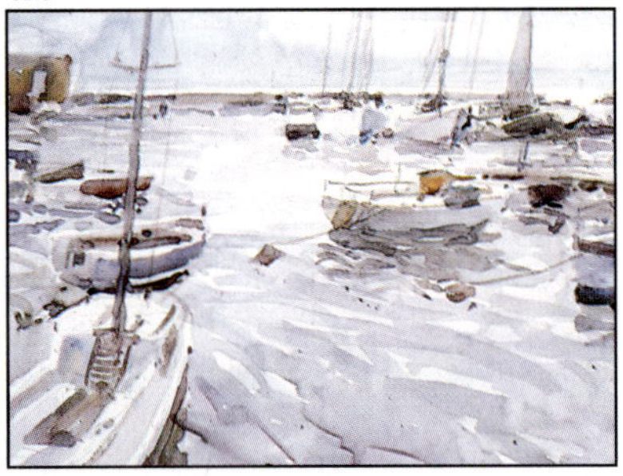

128

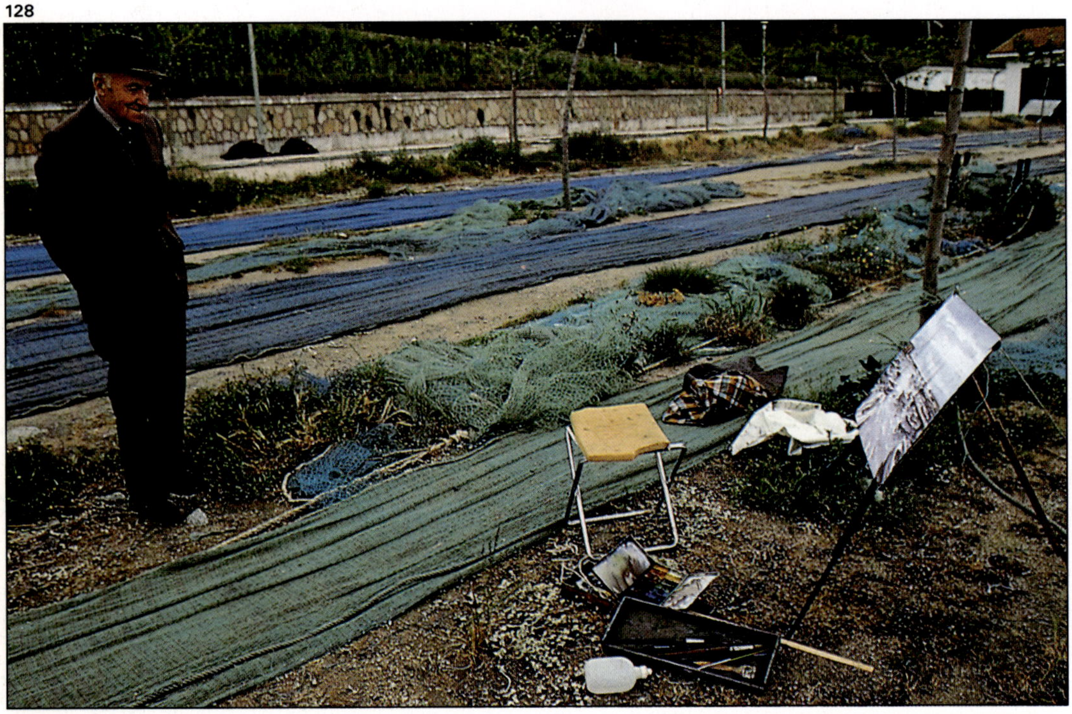

Fig. 126. Each new step implies an overall review, a revision of all the zones of the picture. The boats have captured the painter's attention; their shapes need to be more clearly defined.

Fig. 127. Olivé has shown himself throughout to be a painter who exercises a firm control over his paints, though not too strict a control. At times, as now in the foreground, he allows himself to "play" with the paint.

Fig. 128. As you may already know, it is a good idea to take a short break in any painting session. It is advisable to rest a little, but also to take time out to think and to assess your progress.

Our painter now feels that the time has come to take a look at his work from a distance. He steps back until he is about ten feet from it and, for the first time (fig. 128), seems to meditate on his work.

This meditative inspection makes him think, for example, that he should outline one of the boats in the center more clearly, darken parts of the yacht in the foreground to make the white stand out more, and paint the life buoys hanging from the side of the boat on the far right-hand side. His gaze falls on this right-hand side and he states, "It's too clean, I'll have to put some more rubbish there."

So he begins to paint in some sticks, but pauses after a while to say what all painters say when they get to this point, "You've got to know when to stop."

He contemplates his theme. "A few innocents believe that you should put into a picture everything that is there in real life. But it isn't a question of putting in everything you see, for the picture should be better than real life."

He steps back to a distance of thirteen feet once more. He smiles, satisfied with today's child—the child that has slowly been born before our eyes.

Ceferino Olivé thinks there are just two more things to do before this picture is complete, "Sign and erase...."

Fig. 129. Here, you can appreciate the result of Olivé's meditation. With a touch of dark paint, he has outlined one or two of the boats a bit more against the background, creating more contrast. Also, he has added more vertical lines to the right-hand side. All this depicts what is there in real life, but without falling into the trap of making an exact copy.

129

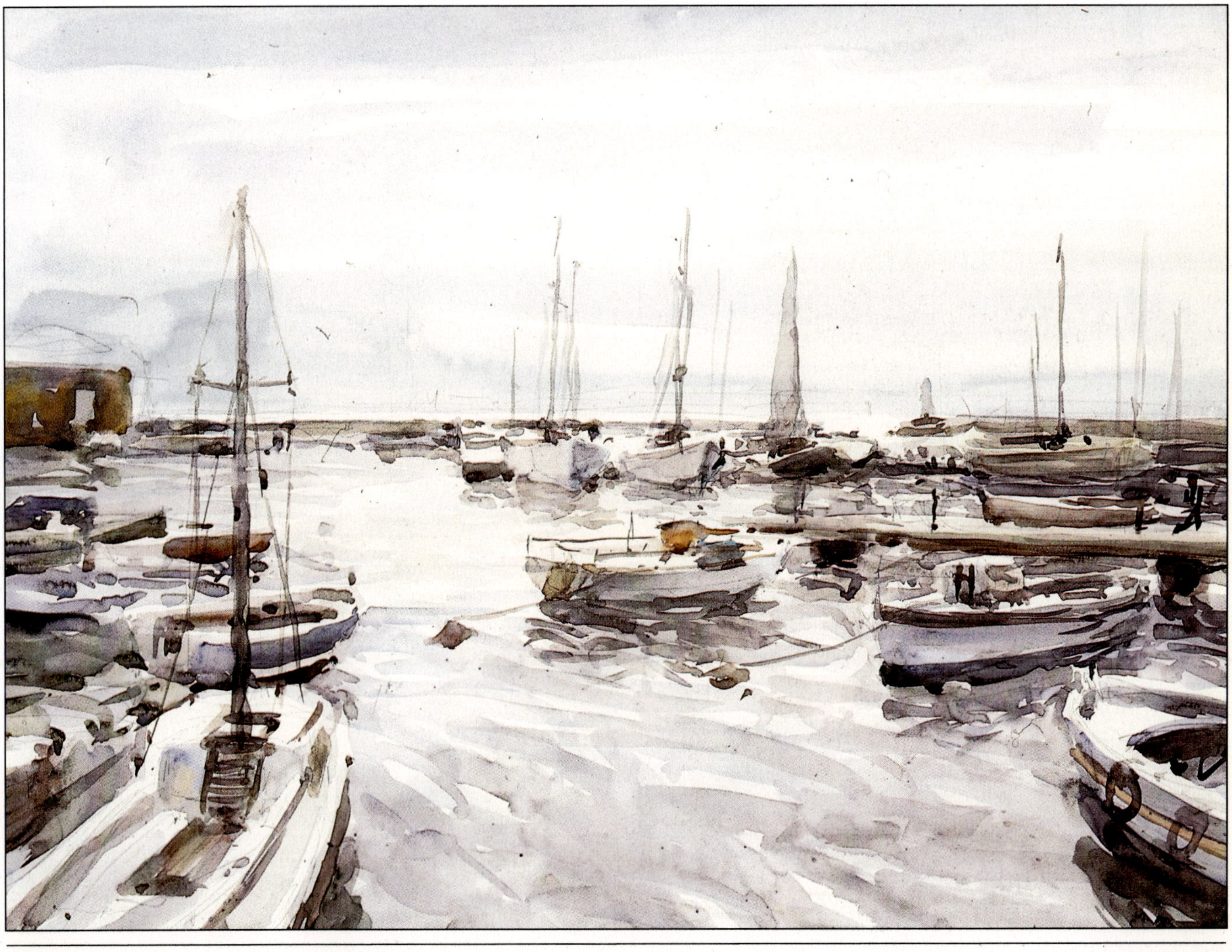

Step five, the last stage: signing and erasing

At this stage, Olivé puts in a few more finishing touches. He darkens the lower part of the sky a bit so that the "fiery" quality of the clear section of the sea will stand out more. He darkens it with a mixture of very dark blue which tends to violet, using a no. 25 brush to paint with. "This will also make the left-hand side vibrate more," he declares proudly.

Now, Olivé only has to sign his work. He does this with distinctive capital letters and adds the date in Roman numerals. "I'm probably the only contemporary painter who puts the date in Roman numerals," he says.

He will let the picture stand for a couple of hours. Then, he will carefully erase the more noticeable pencil lines so that the whites he has left on the paper are cleaner. Once this has been done, the painting can be framed, exhibited, and sold (fig. 132).

130

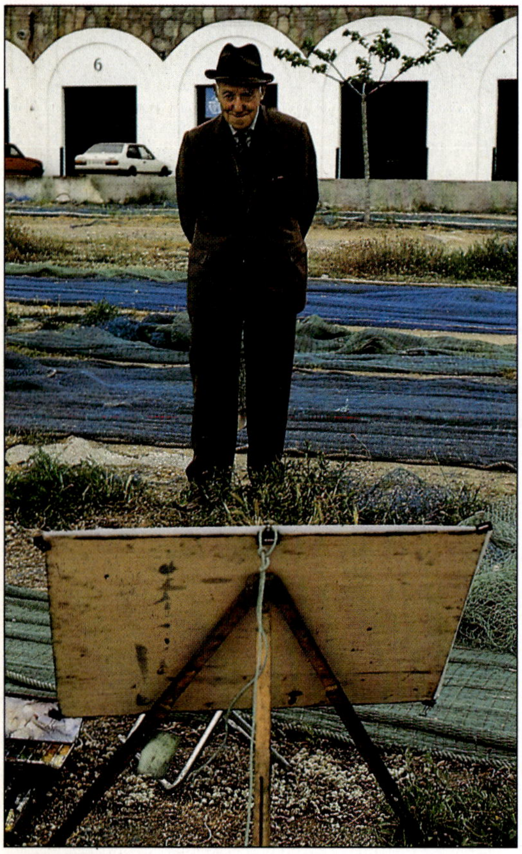

Fig. 130. Ceferino Olivé admires his work with a smile. Moments before, he had been involved in a silent, absorbed examination of his painting. As he had predicted, it took him less than two hours to complete the watercolor. There are still a few last-minute touches to be added, though they are none the less interesting for being the final touches.

Fig. 131. The capital letters and Roman numerals characterizing his signature are not a whim or an eccentricity, but can be seen as confirmation of the faithfulness of Ceferino Olivé to the traditional values, which he maintains and defends.

131

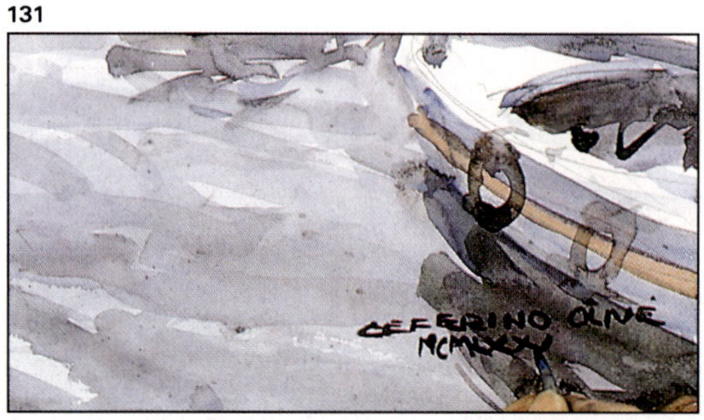

132

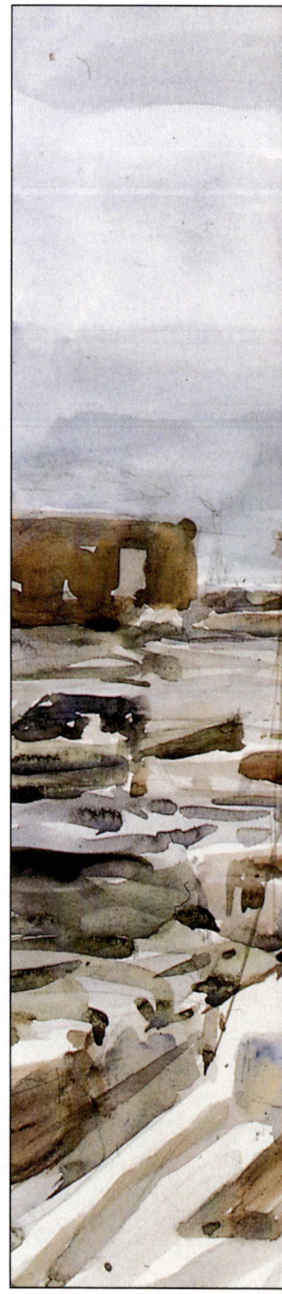

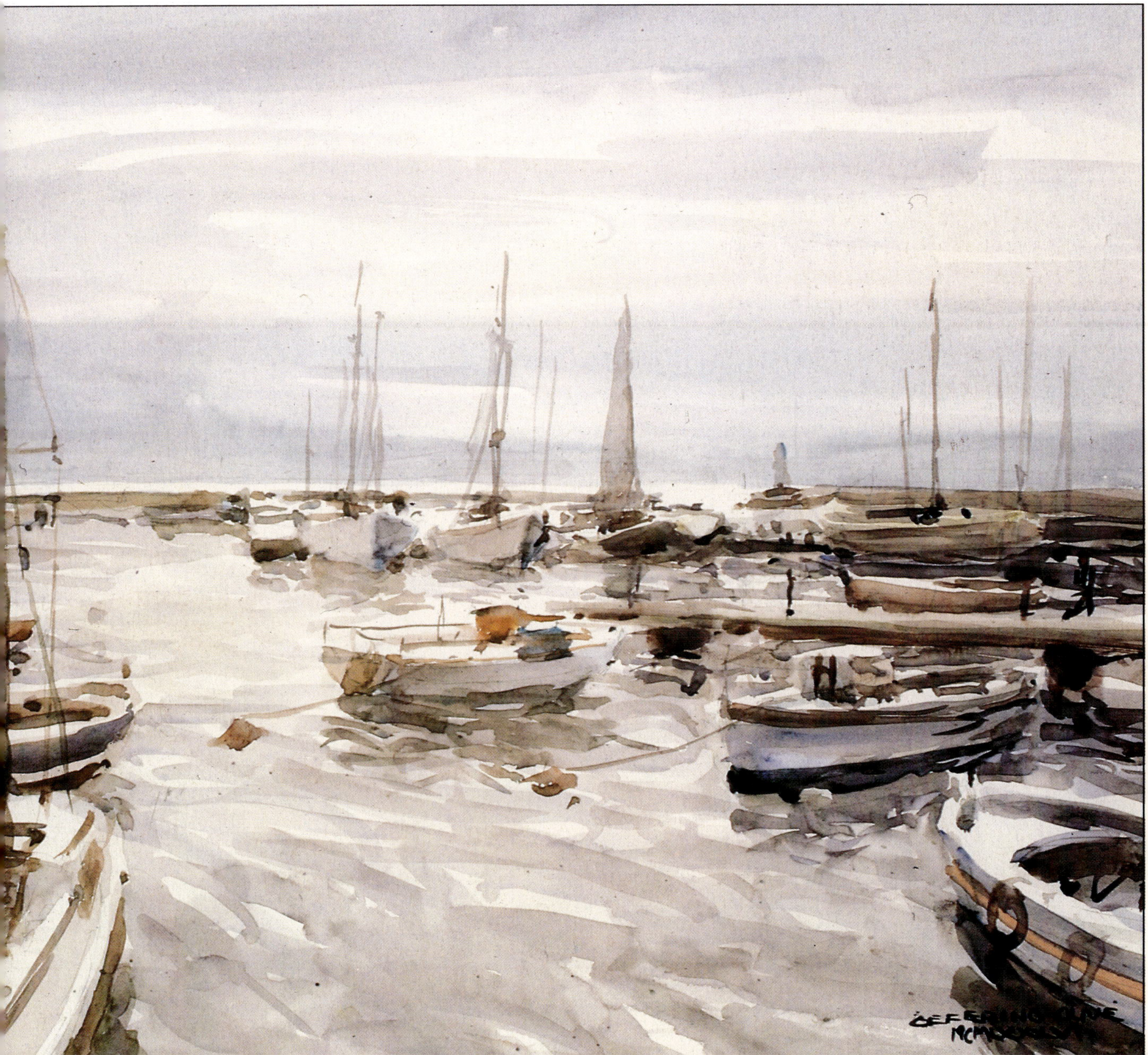

Fig. 132. Five stages have gone into the creation of this watercolor. Starting with the sketch that placed and gave proportion to the elements of this subject, Olivé has worked at the whole painting at once, adjusting and enriching with his successive layers of paint.

The stage of contemplation and meditation has given way to this last step, which is looser and more relaxed. A few brushstrokes were added to the lower part of the sky to provide a lively, vibrant color that gives personality to the work of Ceferino Olivé.

Preparation

On a sunny winter's day, driven by Vicenç Ballestar, we go out to a place on the coast. Here, we discover a small group of rocks which, though only a short distance from some abandoned factories, still have the look of a wild, deserted coastline.

This is the subject that Vicenç Ballestar has decided to paint for us (fig. 134). You could not say that it is a new theme in the history of painting. There are good examples of the treatment of the same theme in the work of Courbet, Monet, or even Cézanne. This subject is, however, original if you consider the usual themes depicted in the seascape.

The right point of view

Ballestar, who knows this spot well and often comes to paint here, starts to look for a good position among the rocks. He explores the whole area, jumping with agility from rock to rock.

Our guest painter decides it is best to wait a while until the sun is higher, as the backlighting at this time of day is very strong.

Eventually, we find the most suitable position to avoid the violent effects of the backlighting.

"I'm particularly fond of backlighting," Ballestar says. "But the picture would perhaps be too much a collection of dark stains." He would prefer to paint something more instructive—something the reader can learn more from—and we are grateful to him for this.

Setting up the materials

Ballestar places his portable paintbox on top of a rock, in what we must say is a rather precarious position. Fortunately, there is hardly any wind today to upset it.

He has mounted his Schöller medium-grain paper on a no. 12 wedged stretcher. Then, he supports the stretcher on a drawing board; otherwise the light shining through would make it impossible for him to identify his colors. At any rate, Ballestar has positioned himself in such a way that the sun does not shine directly onto his paper.

133

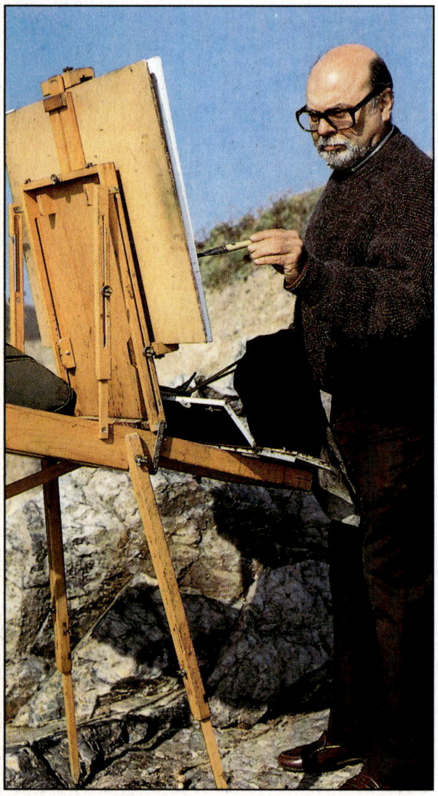

Fig. 133. Ballestar has total concentration on his work as he paints in the open air. Real life, in his opinion, has enormous advantages over painting in the studio.

134

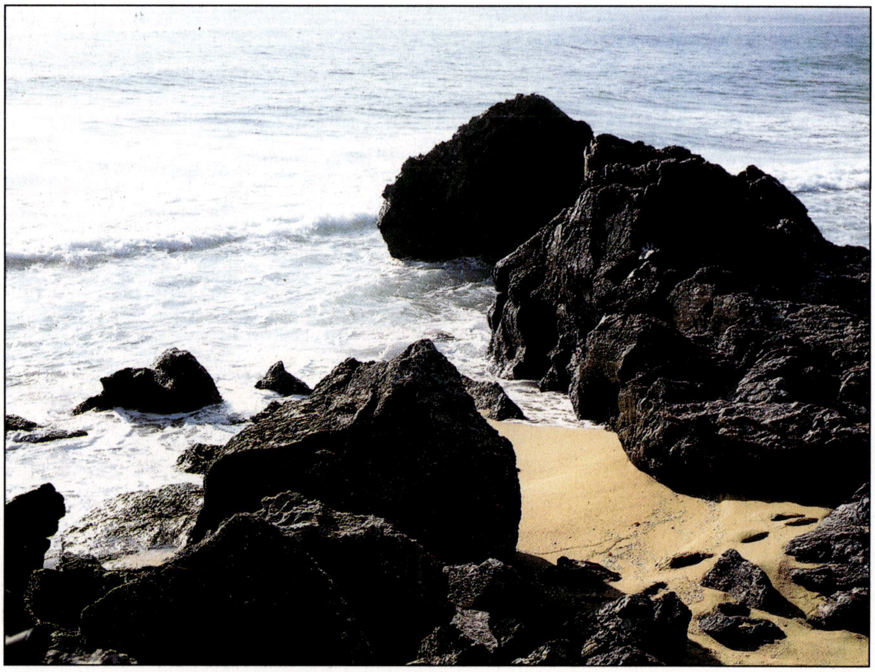

Fig. 134. The most unexpected places can supply ideal subjects for painting; it is a question of imagination and the correct use of resources such as framing, point of view, and composition. In this case, Ballestar has transformed this group of rocks, nearby to an industrial zone, into an attractive, solitary coastline.

The work of Vicenç Ballestar

135

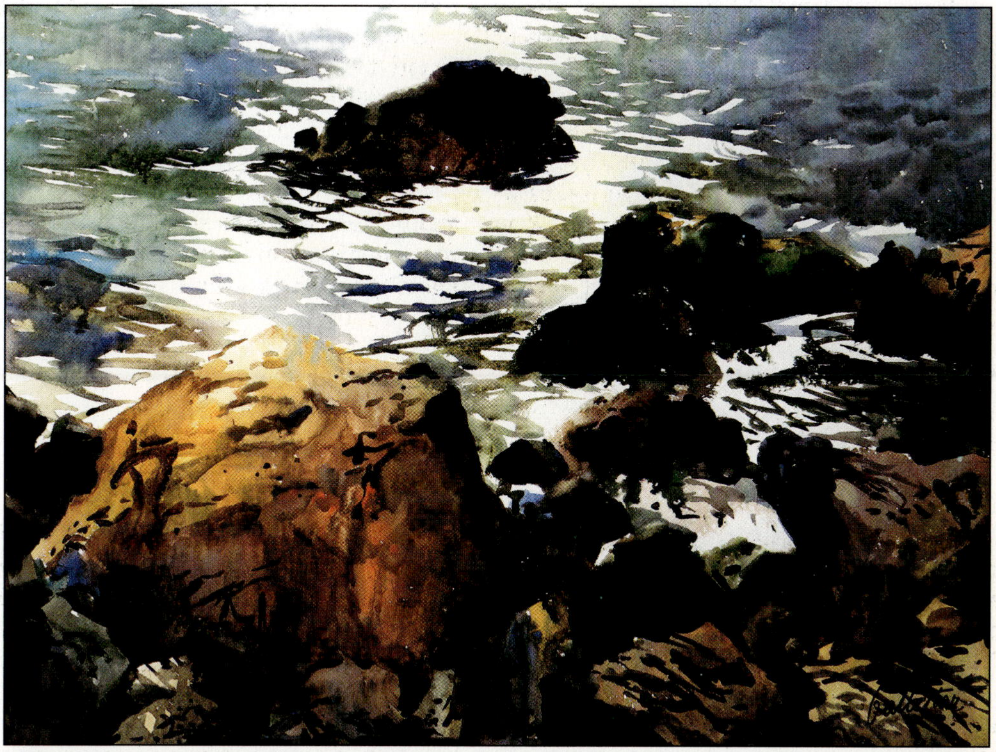

136

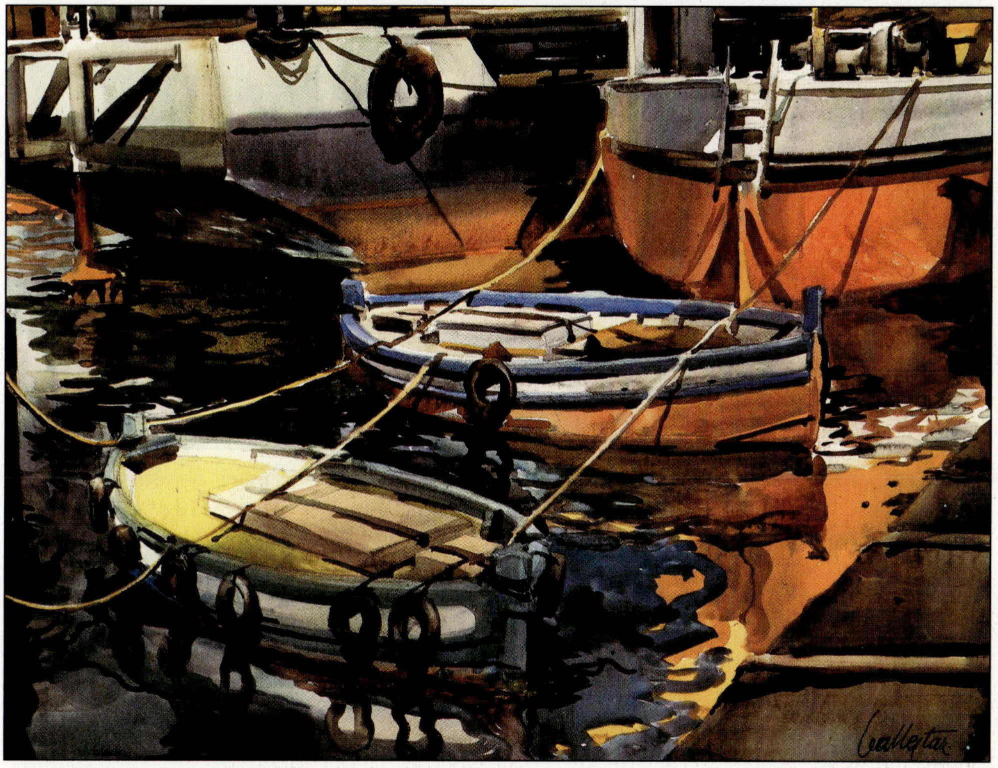

Figs. 135 and 136. The seascape is a frequent theme in the work of this prolific painter, but it is not the only one by any means. Paintings of animals and figures also make up a large portion of his work.

Ballestar continually strives to find new solutions, new possibilities for subjects such as the seascape; this is an evident aspect in the work of Ballestar. His "rock seascapes," as we could call them (fig. 135) are certainly individual, though not completely unknown, themes. He does not, however, reject more common themes for a seascape, such as a view of a port as seen in figure 136. In these paintings, the artist reveals his penchant for taking risks and his rich use of color, rejecting detail to concentrate on truly pictorial problems.

Drawing

Ballestar speaks of the pleasure of painting in the open air. "Painting from real life gives you experience and suggestions that don't come to you when you're painting from a photo, in which there is no movement." He expresses his ideas enthusiastically, with great vitality.

The first thing Ballestar does is study his composition, moving his finger over the white paper. Then, with a charcoal pencil, he begins to draw his subject. He draws a horizontal line across the top part of the paper. Ballestar alternates between using the flat part and the tip of the charcoal to draw in the lines of the rocks.

He completes the sketch, reproduced in figure 137, with great speed. Drawing and erasing with a rag, correcting and adjusting the silhouettes, he explains that he does not want to do a detailed sketch. He just wants to "place the theme." The framing he has chosen is striking. Unlike other seascapes, where the sky has a fundamental weight in the picture, Ballestar has centered his attention on the rocks, even reducing the presence of the sea as far as possible.

Paint and brushes

Now, Ballestar prepares the seven brushes he is going to paint with. There are two flat brushes; one sow-hair brush used for oil painting, which he uses to remove excess water; two round no. 7 brushes; a round *petit-gris* which, in his words, "absorbs a lot of water"; and, lastly, the smallest brush of all, also a round brush. Ballestar uses a paintbox with a double top (fig. 138); it contains a range of sixteen colors: lemon yellow, cadmium orange, vermillion, carmine, burnt carmine, several blues, ultramarine blue, cobalt blue, cerulean blue, permanent blue light, ochre, burnt sienna, Van Dyck brown, bottle green, olive green, and emerald green, which he uses to darken indigo. "I also use Naples yellow to tinge my yellows, an oxide red that combines well with ochres, and mauve, which I mix with complementary colors," he adds.

The last step in his preparation is to fill a small plastic pot with water, but, strangely, mineral water! Ballestar sees the surprise on our faces, and explains, "For a hundred pesetas, you can have a drink, which you may need later on...."

Fig. 137. The choice of the right framing and point of view are two fundamental steps that have to be taken into consideration before you begin to paint. Ballestar, for example, has taken up a position a little higher than the group of rocks, concentrating his attention almost exclusively on them. His framing limits the presence of the sea to a minimum, making the rocks his central theme.

Fig. 138. Laid out on the ground near to his easel, we can see the brushes he is going to use.

Fig. 139. His first brushstrokes form a strange crisscross pattern of lines through which the white of the paper can still be seen.

137

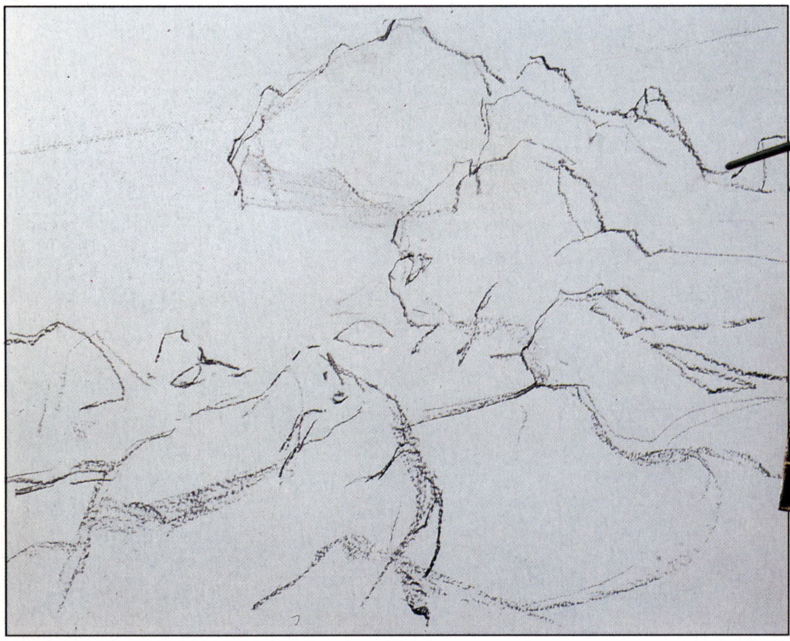

138

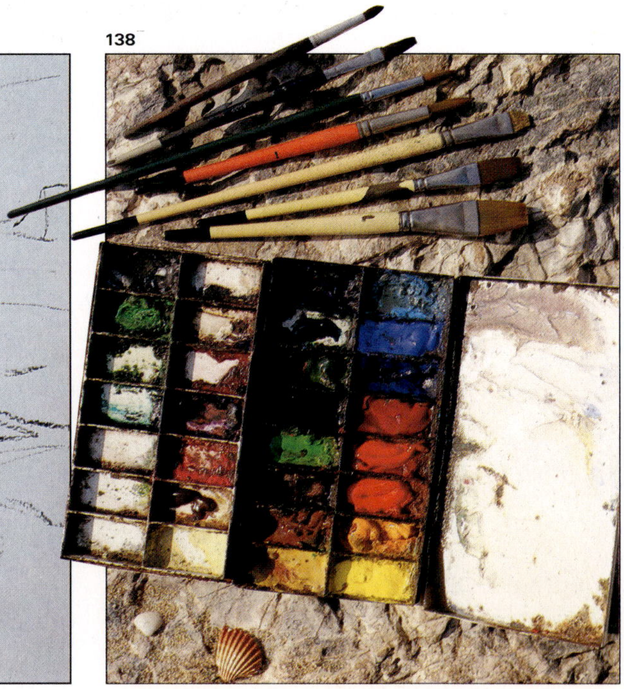

Step one: defining areas of color

Fig. 140. To paint the sea, he allows the bluish and greenish tones of the watercolor to spread freely over the paper. In places, he absorbs excess paint with his brush.

Fig. 141. With a deep ochre, he paints the beach. His parallel, concave strokes set a rhythm that is intent on completing the composition.

Fig. 142. This is an overall view of Ballestar's sketch. The three areas of color define his working guidelines: the sea, the most distant rock, and the beach in the foreground.

The first stains Ballestar paints on the paper appear in the sea. They are strokes of a greenish color, a mixture of emerald green, cobalt blue, and cerulean blue. Ballestar has an unusual way of using his brush, spreading the paint but also picking it up and making his colors lighter with it. He cleans his palette with the flat brush, too, shaking it out afterward onto the ground. He mixes ultramarine blue and green again and paints the resulting color over the previous layer, using crisscross strokes to create a pattern (fig. 139). He leaves the area he has been painting for a while, takes up his palette again, and mixes a little violet with sienna and brown, also adding a spot of green and blue to paint the most distant rocks. Ballestar points out the importance of using a wide range of tones, to enrich colors so that "when the painting is dry it doesn't all look the same, or uniform." In fact, Ballestar is producing an extraordinary concentration of colors in a limited space.

He goes back to the sea, and with cerulean blue light he paints in a slightly inclined horizontal strip over his earlier charcoal line. He allows the paint to form drops and run a little, creating random effects. But he also works on the runs, placing them with the brush or absorbing some of their color. He paints quickly, without pause (fig. 140). "At the beginning, it's hard to stop," he says.

Ballestar begins to work on the foreground now, covering the sandy area with a deep yellowish ochre, highly saturated. First, he paints a rectangular stain to which he adds a dark, umber color. Subsequent brushstrokes create concave lines, enclosing and emphasizing the diagonal line of the composition (fig. 141).

"I like to have one color in the background," he comments, "another making a stronger contrast, and a last one approaching the foreground; three areas of color that give me the overall sense of my work." We can see what he means in figure 142.

He continues, "If you start work on the background and then move toward the foreground, you could make mistakes that can't later be put right." This consideration should be kept in mind, especially when painting in a medium such as watercolor, with which there is no going back.

139

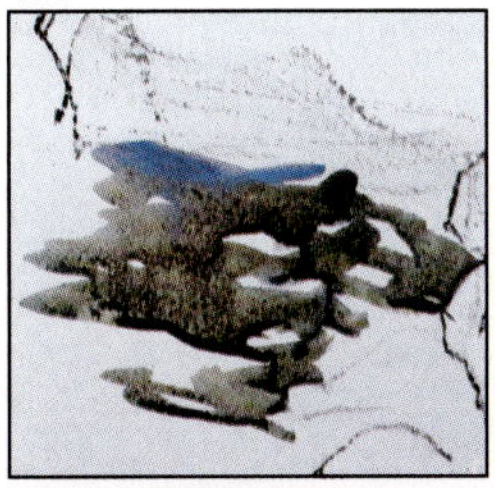

140

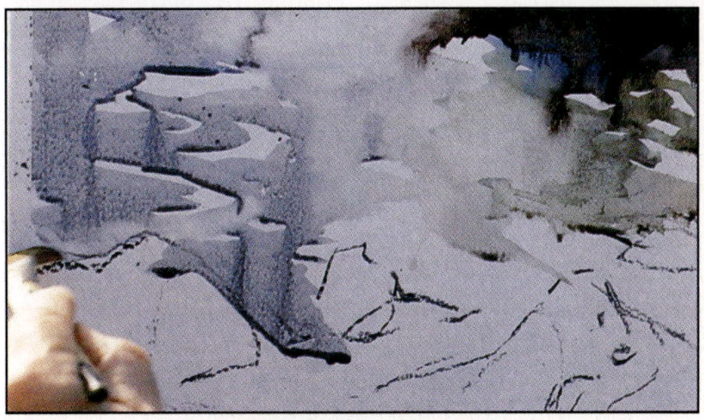

141

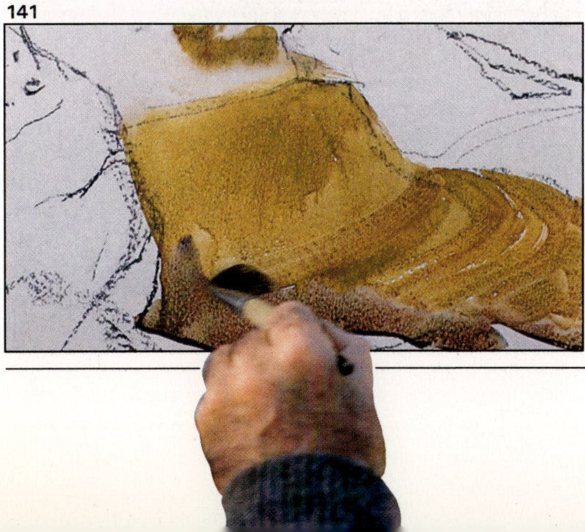

142

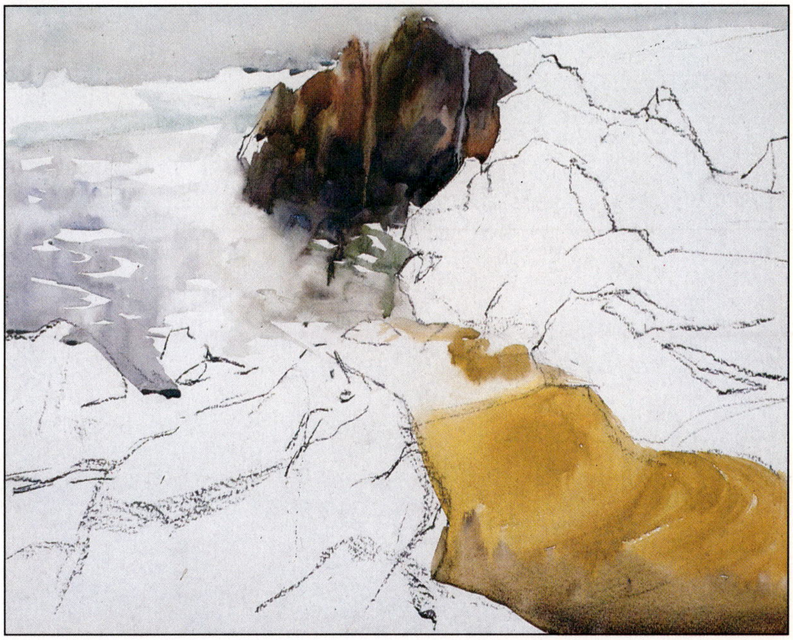

Step two: defining the overall picture

Ballestar gives us more and more clues to understanding his concept of painting. "I generally paint a stain and then stretch it across the paper, partly because I prefer to mix colors on the paper rather than on the palette. That way I feel I get a more consistent, more solid color."

And this is exactly what he does when painting the shadow, or shadows, of the rock on the left-hand side (fig. 143). Deep carmines and blues, with an occasional touch of indigo, give shape to the different planes forming the rock.

Ballestar now makes this important comment: "It is essential to enrich color at the first attempt, to use color directly rather than deepen it little by little." This is the best way to paint in watercolor; it is the one where painters commit themselves the most.

"I don't use the same method all the time; I just seize the moment when I see clearly what I should do," he adds. Practicing what he preaches, Ballestar now moves to the right-hand side of the picture. To complete the lower part of the beach he makes a uniform, soft, stumped stain, using a warm, broken tone.

He goes back to the sea once more. With the same crisscross strokes as before, he expands out toward the left, still using a green, but this time a lighter tone (fig. 144). Then, he applies a dirty ochre on the right-hand side of the rock with short, broad brushstrokes.

Next, the artist paints in two small rocks. At this stage, it is interesting to see how, from the start, he bears in mind the appearance the rocks should have, continuously bathed by the unrelenting sea.

"When I paint," he says, "I use the white of the paper, leaving it as it is, to try to capture the effect of the sea on the rock." This is another feature of watercolor, the fact that you can use the tone of the paper to express lights or shines.

Fig. 144. Painting the entire surface in one session is the technique that commits the painter the most. Tone is usually produced by applying various layers of paint that progress from light to dark, but Ballestar prefers to apply his colors directly, without intermediary stages.

Fig. 145. Painting these rocks is like painting a small jigsaw puzzle of planes. Along with the colors used, it is also important to take care over the direction of the brushstrokes, which helps to define volume more clearly.

Fig. 146. Ballestar reserves several white areas in this puzzle, over which he will later paint the lighter colors of the rocks. But for the moment, he concentrates on the darker colors, the shadows, though he does not always paint in this order.

143

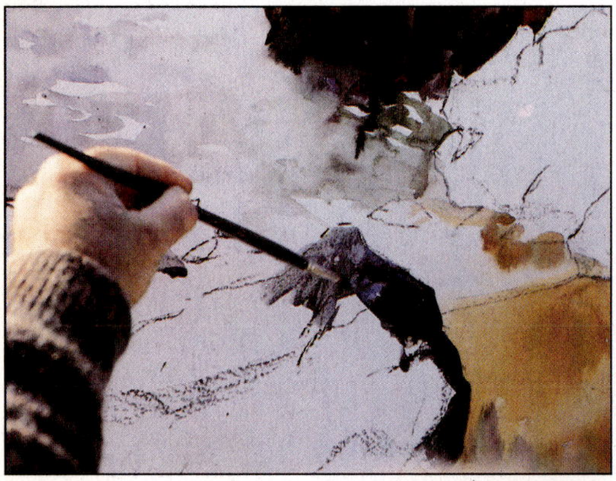

144

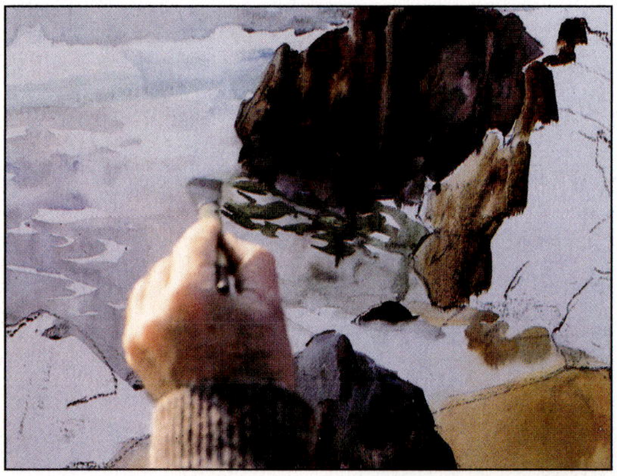

Fig. 143. Colors are usually mixed on the palette, but Ballestar prefers to perform this operation on the paper itself—"stretching" the stains.

145

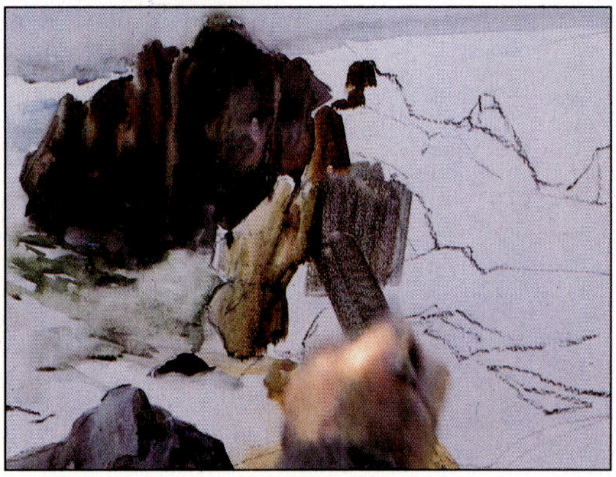

146

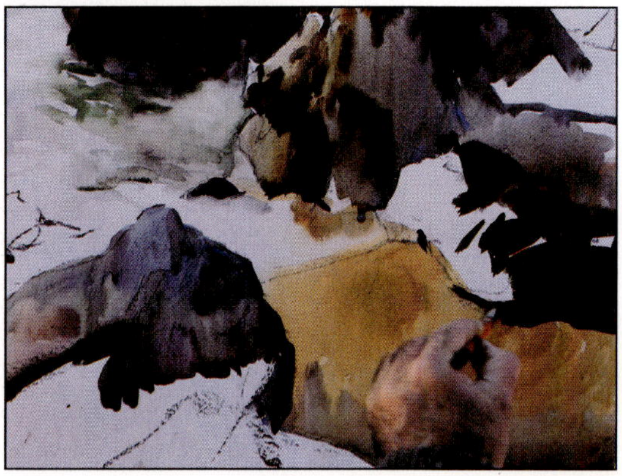

Ballestar now decides to continue working on the group of rocks on the right, painting them with a mauve color mixed with carmine and sienna. First, he applies various parallel strokes, all in the same direction. Then, he changes their angle to make them slope to the right, as you can see in figure 145. He paints with vigorous, impatient strokes. "Right from the start, I always want to see results, things on my paper," Ballestar explains.

His brushstrokes continue to be inspired by a burning desire for definition—a shadow in ultramarine blue, now a little brown, then another stain of a broken tone. He always paints within a range of very rich colors to avoid the hardness, the uniformity of the shadows when the paint is dry.

Ballestar is very clear in his views about the role of color. "It's more a case of suggesting than of analyzing color by color. The final result should, as far as possible, express what I feel." Sometimes, however, even an idea that is completely clear to us does not give the expected results. Normally, Ballestar does not paint light and shade in any predetermined order. Instead, he paints first one and then the other and vice versa, allowing his inspiration to guide him. Now, he paints fresh shadows on the rocks with carmine, brown, and bottle green, leaving the areas touched by the light white, to be painted later (fig. 146).

Little by little, the painting acquires the appearance of a mosaic of skillfully placed colors. Ballestar has kept us constantly aware of the dangers of taking on a subject such as this, where it is all too easy to fall into the trap of detail and preciousness. To avoid falling into this trap, he paints with stains to define the planes that, in turn, give form to the subject (fig. 147).

147

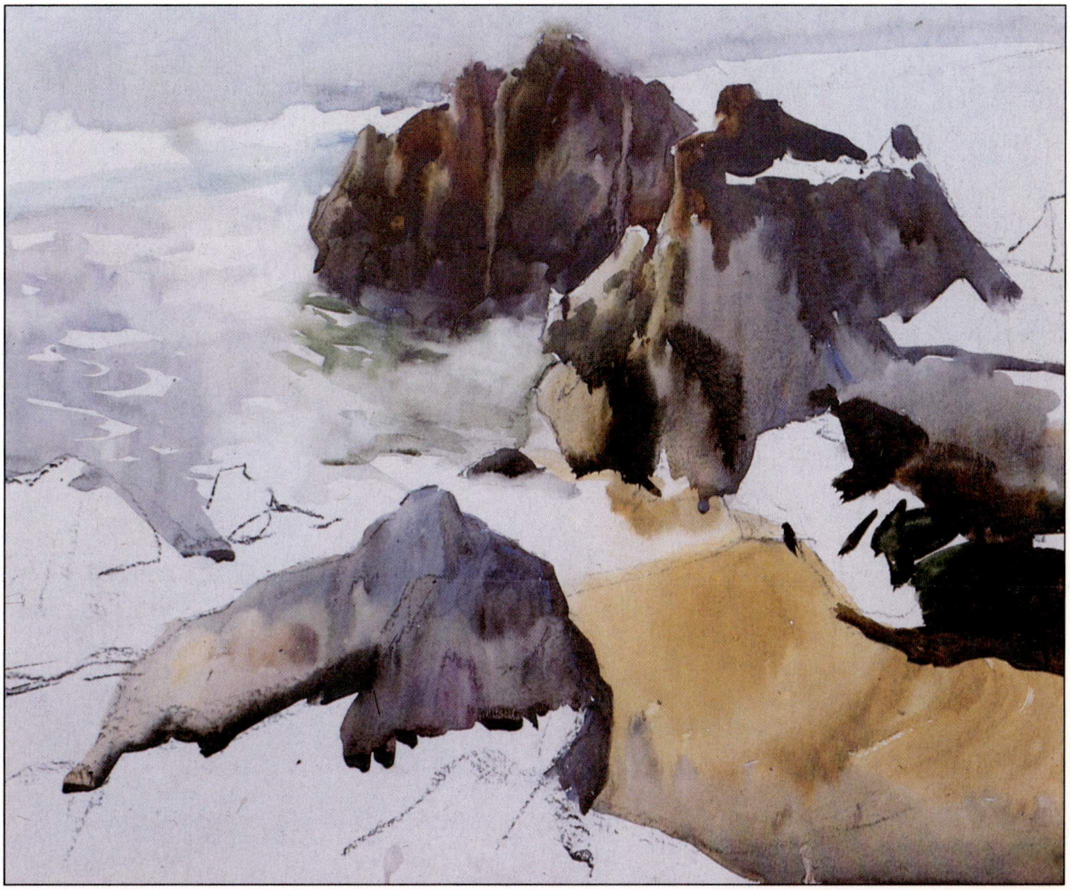

Fig. 147. New colors have gradually appeared on the paper, in the same way that new notes are added to a melody—in complete harmony with the work as a whole. For the moment, low notes, dark colors within a rich range, predominate this composition.

Step three: adjustments

"First, I stain everything; then I adjust it." With these words, Ballestar announces one of the most delicate moments in any session of painting. The painter, once he has completed the general or overall work, has to know instinctively when and where to stop, which is always difficult.

Ballestar decides to work on the group of rocks to the left first, a group surrounded by the sea like a small archipelago. Here, he paints four intensely colored stains with a very dark sienna (fig. 148). The artist reminds us that "you have to do with water what water does." Then, he takes his *petit-gris* brush, dips it only in water, and creates the effect of water splashing against the painted rocks. He spreads and absorbs the paint until he achieves the effect he wants (fig. 149).

After a brief pause in which he steps back a few steps to examine the picture as a whole, Ballestar tells us about the pictorial effect he is seeking to create. "I'm trying to suggest things with as much simplicity as possible, synthesizing, for example, all those cracks in the rocks."

With a warm dark gray, a mixture of the three primary colors, yellow, carmine, and ultramarine blue, he paints over the dry ochre-colored base. Then, he paints the shadow cast by the rocks onto the beach (fig. 150).

This same color, to which he now adds a little olive green, he uses to suggest shadows reflected in the water. With just four brushtrokes, he gives a magnificent example of his graphic skills, as you can appreciate in figure 151.

Ballestar is careful not to overdo it. His paper is becoming softer, due to the dampness in the air, and this can reduce his control of the paint.

He now centers his attention on the sea, painting several lines in the top right-hand section with cobalt blue (fig. 152). Next, he

148

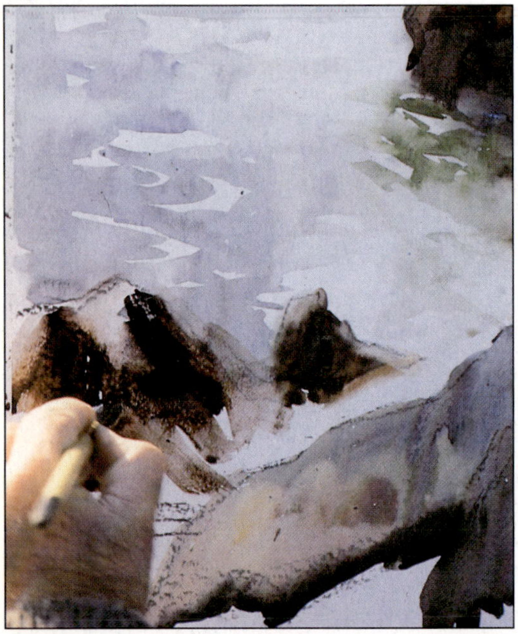

149

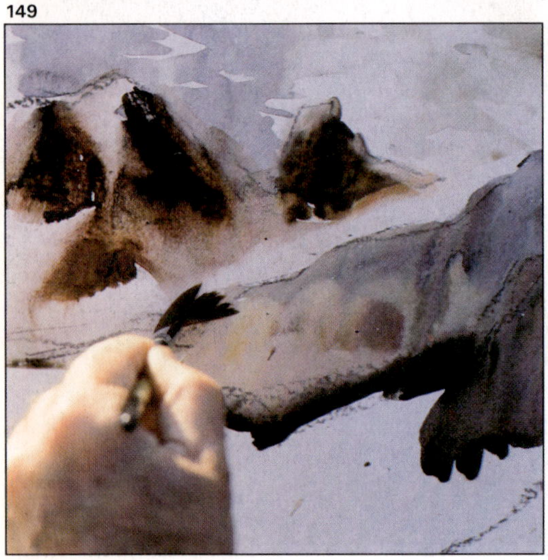

150

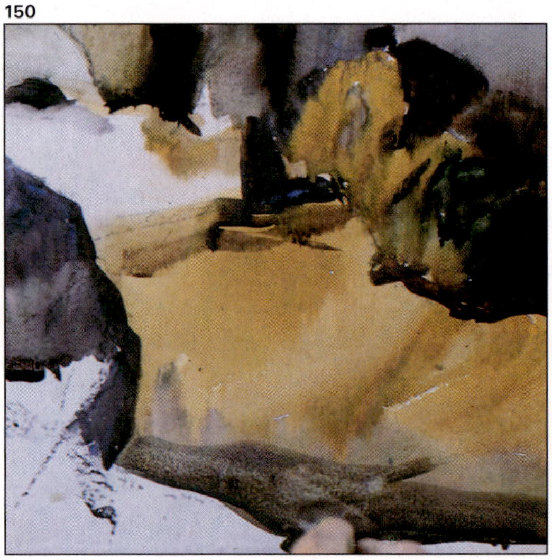

151

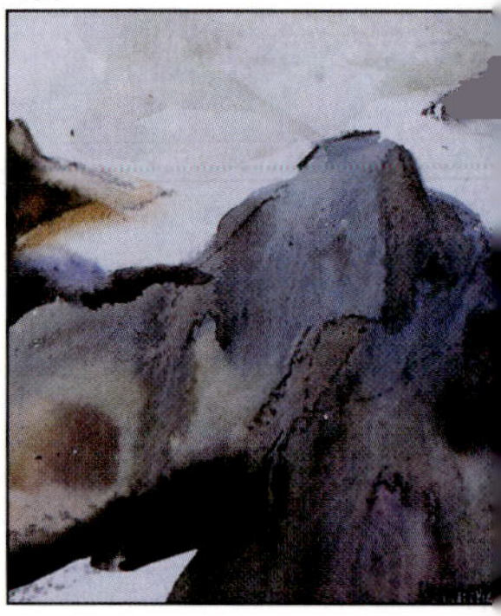

Fig. 148. Staining and then adjusting, that is the method followed in this watercolor. This method requires the stain to be applied decisively, but then carefully adjusted to preserve the original freshness of the painting.

Fig. 149. The *petit-gris* brush dipped in water alone enables Ballestar to "paint" the effect of the sea on the rocks. He uses the white of the paper to represent foam or reflections.

Fig. 150. Occasionally, Ballestar employs traditional watercolor techniques. The shadow of this rock is the result of successive layers of transparent color.

moves over to the left-hand side to paint with ultramarine blue over the light blue base. He applies the paint, then absorbs it back onto his brush. He paints and unpaints, concentrating on the play of transparencies. This is his way of painting.

To finish, he reinforces the strip of cerulean blue with green to make this area stand out against the diagonal line formed by the rocks. Once again, he gives his drops of paint free rein to run as they please, creating new, unforeseen effects (fig. 153). "What I want is to evoke the movement of the sea in a simple way, economically and without overdoing the brushstrokes," he declares.

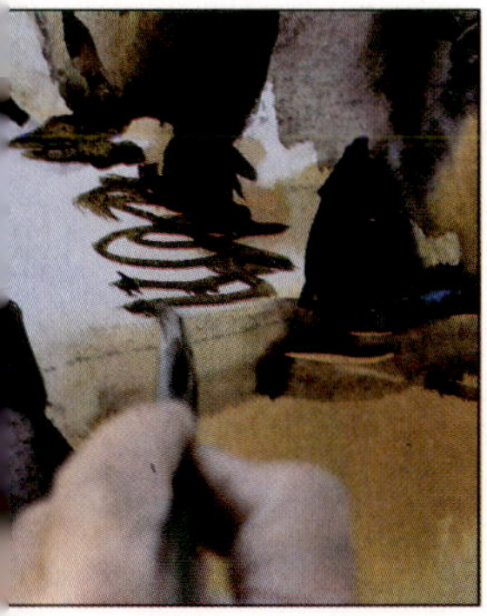

152

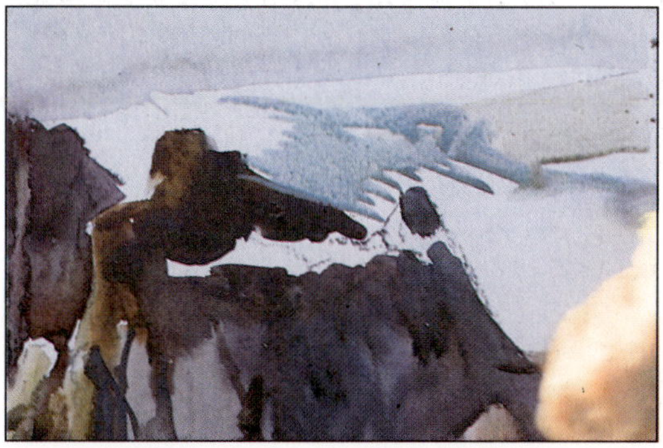

153

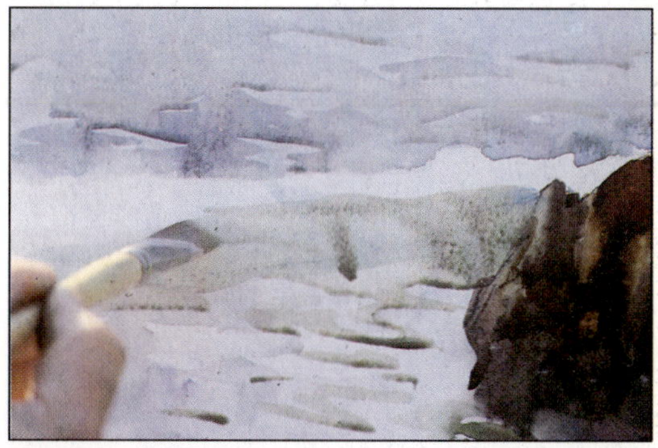

154

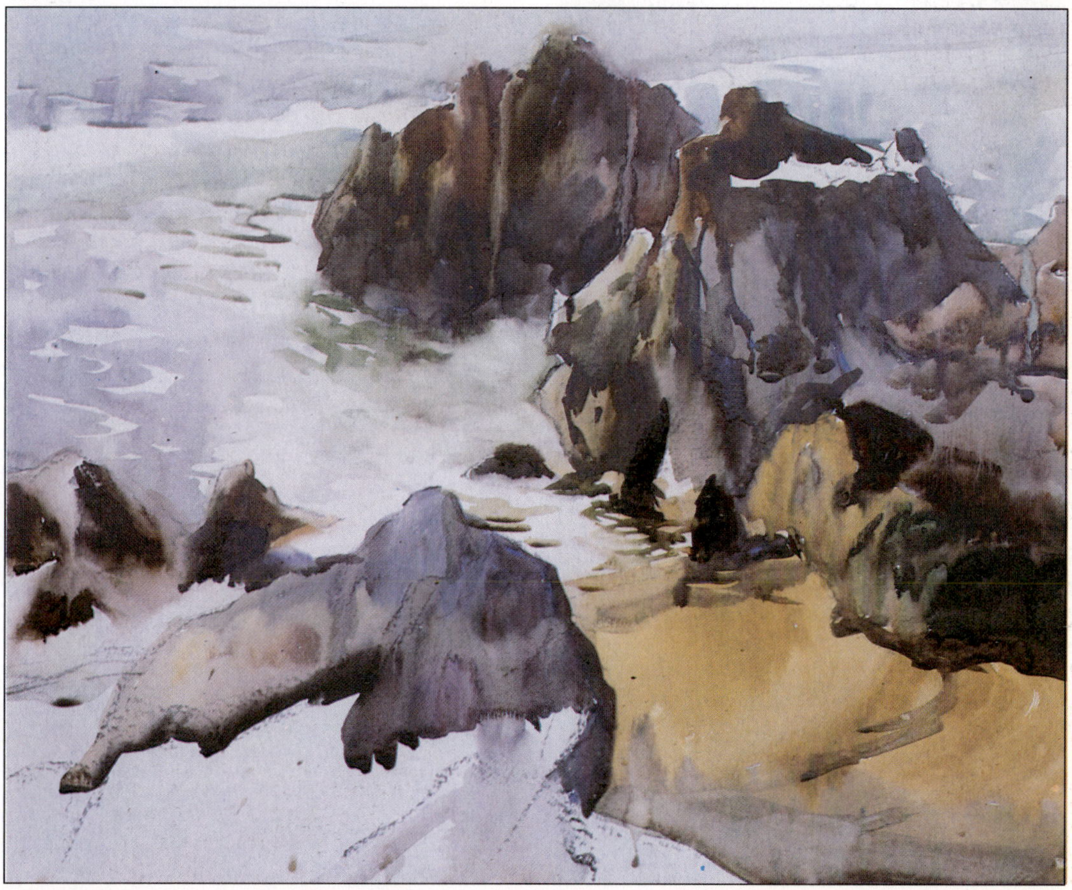

Figs. 151 to 153. One of the most suggestive aspects for the seascape painter is the variety of effects of the light on the constantly moving surface of the sea. This is the painter's opportunity to demonstrate his resources. In figure 151, Ballestar has painted a shadow *alla prima*; in the next figure, he has used a peculiar zigzag line; and in the last figure, he has applied a subtle greenish wash to emphasize the white diagonal line by the foam of the sea.

Fig. 154. Do not overpaint, let your picture breathe. Know when to stop. All this requires great wisdom and mastery. At such an advanced stage as this, the tone of each brushstroke must be carefully calculated and left to dry a little so as not to lose control over the rest of the painting.

Step four: painting over the last whites

155

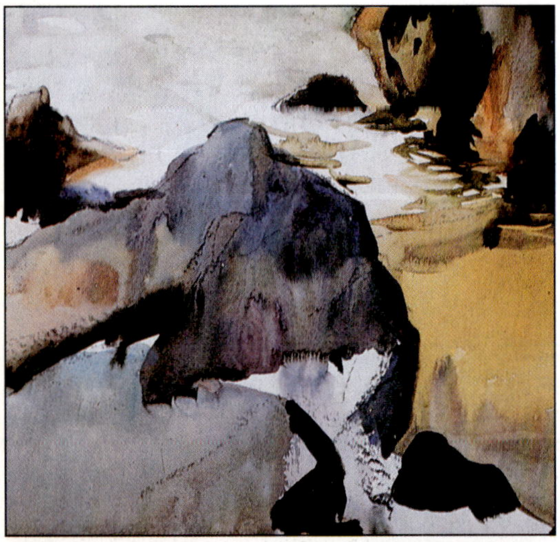

156

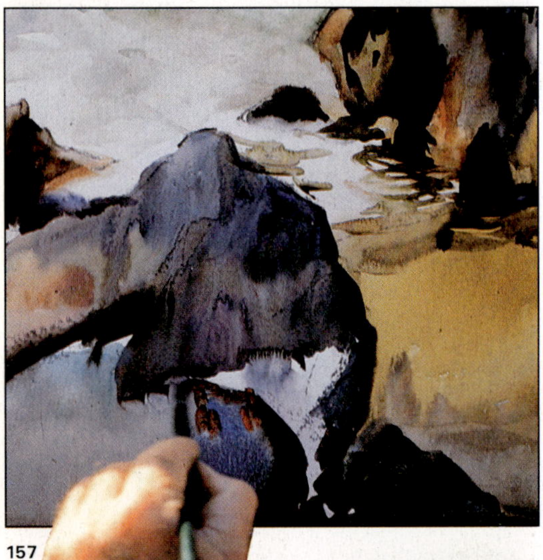

157

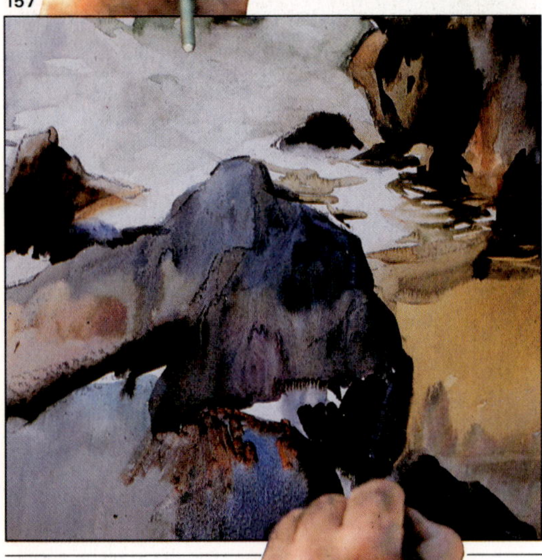

158

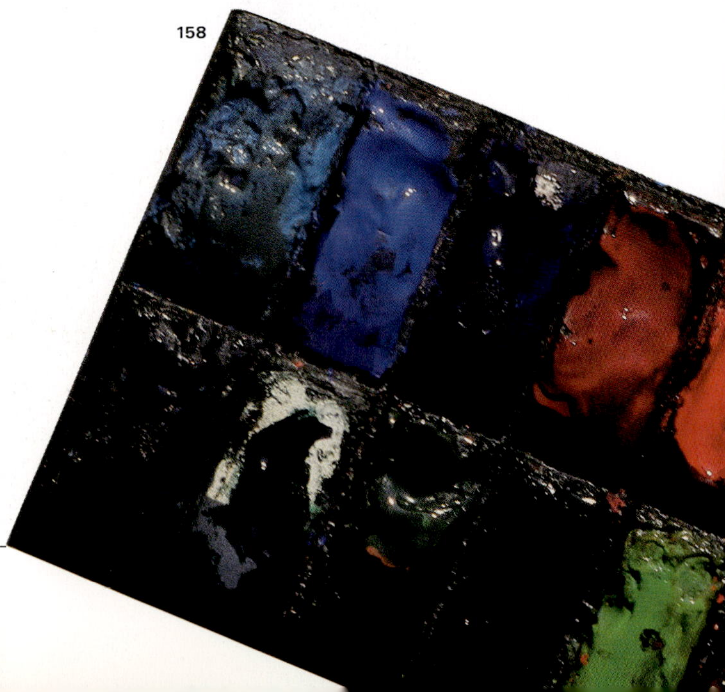

If it is generally true that you can see the relationship between one particular type of painting and its author, in this case we could say that the painter and his painting are intimately related. Ballestar's tremendous vitality and his eternal good humor are expressed to perfection in the chromatic richness, brilliance, and energetic brushstrokes of his work.

We should add a third quality to this list: his ability to hold onto a clear vision of the overall work and to harmonize a wide variety of tones in his painting, which he does by working on the picture as a whole.

In this next stage, though, he will concentrate his attention on the rock in the foreground nearest to us. This is the only place on the paper where the white of the paper still shows through.

Ballestar, with blue and green stains, constructs various planes in shadow. We are impressed by the sureness and lightness of hand the artist demonstrates. His brush glides over the paper as if each stroke responds immediately to his desire. The truth is, though, that this is the fruit of years of experience.

Though Ballestar continues painting the same rock, from time to time he also discovers other parts of the picture that deserve his attention. For example, the beach, where an umber tone reinforces the shadow cast by the rock, or the group of rocks on the

Fig. 155. Ballestar has alternately painted one section and then another, so that the whole picture progresses at the same time. Nevertheless, there are still some white areas on which he now centers his attention. Given his mastery in the harmonization of different tones and hues, these white areas will not pose a great problem.

Fig. 156. In the hand of this painter, the brush acquires a remarkable facility to respond to his desires. Each stroke, straight, curved, or broken, fits into its place with precision and spontaneity; thus confirming the ability and experience of Ballestar.

Figs. 157 and 158. These dense, dark tones, tending to blue and green, are used to construct different shaded planes on the rock.

Fig. 159. The paintbrush, in the right hands, can produce a rich range of strokes and stains. The tip of a flat brush, for example, can be used to obtain effects like these, simulating cracks. Really, they are lines that give greater variety to the flat brushstrokes that predominate this section of the painting.

Fig. 160. A look at Ballestar's palette confirms our earlier intuition that we are witnessing a splendid exercise in color. Using a variety of colors, Ballestar has obtained a rich mosaic of tones and hues which, despite their number and quality, do not adversely affect the overall harmony of his picture in the slightest.

right, forming a diagonal line that Ballestar feels stands out too much. To soften this effect, he paints just the tip of another rock, placing it to the right of this group, giving continuity to the subtle horizon on the sea.

But he returns immediately to the rock he is concerned with. So deep in concentration is he, that the explanations which have flowed freely from him until now become scarcer. We do not dare press him with our questions.

He is still working with the flat brush, though using only the tip. He paints a series of short, dark strokes that suggest the cracks and grooves in the rock.

It is not a question of getting carried away by detail, as he himself has pointed out before. You have to distinguish between the pictorial, the problem of color and form, and what is picturesque and precious. "Things that I totally reject," the artist firmly states.

Ballestar finishes by covering the lower part of the rock with a number of short brushstrokes, one next to the other, painting in an upward direction. More than a finish, this is a base over which he will paint over again, once it has dried.

159

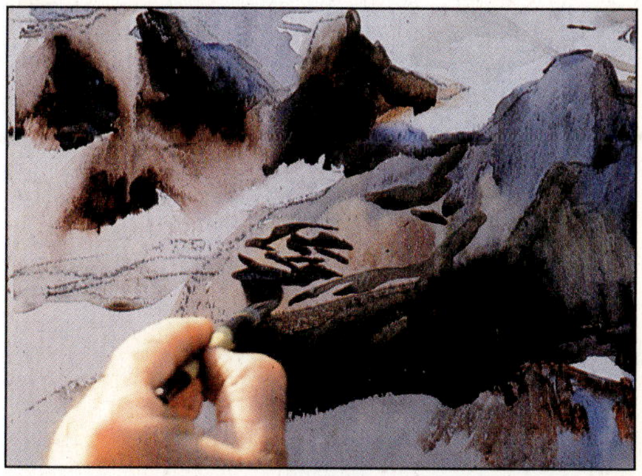

160

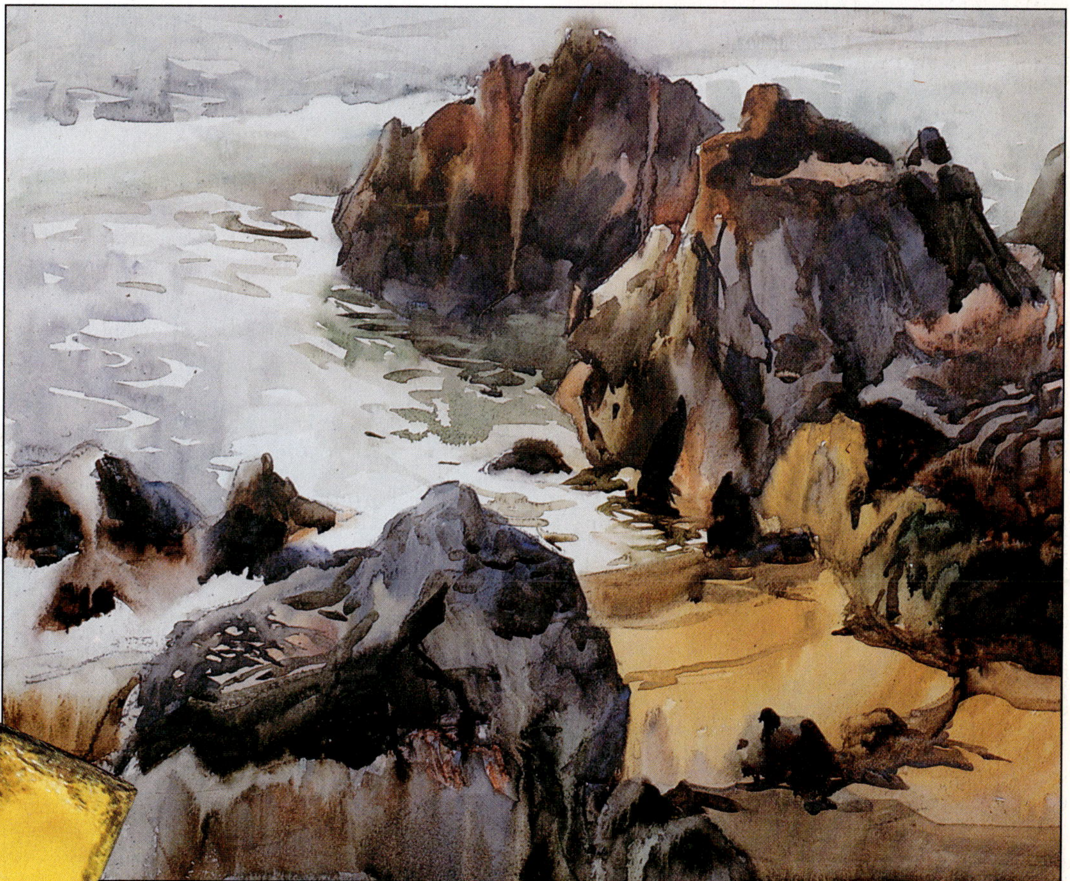

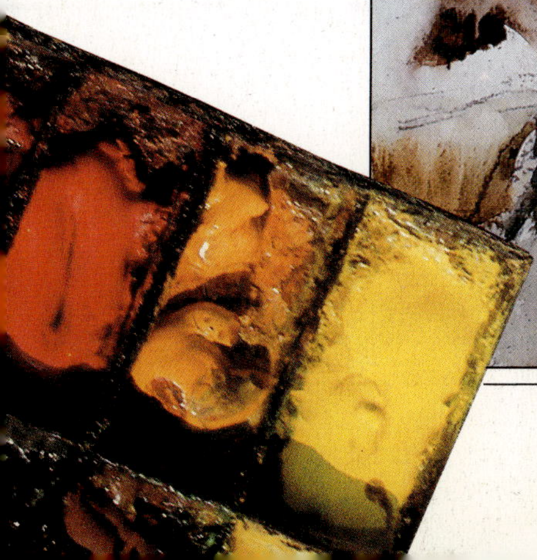

161

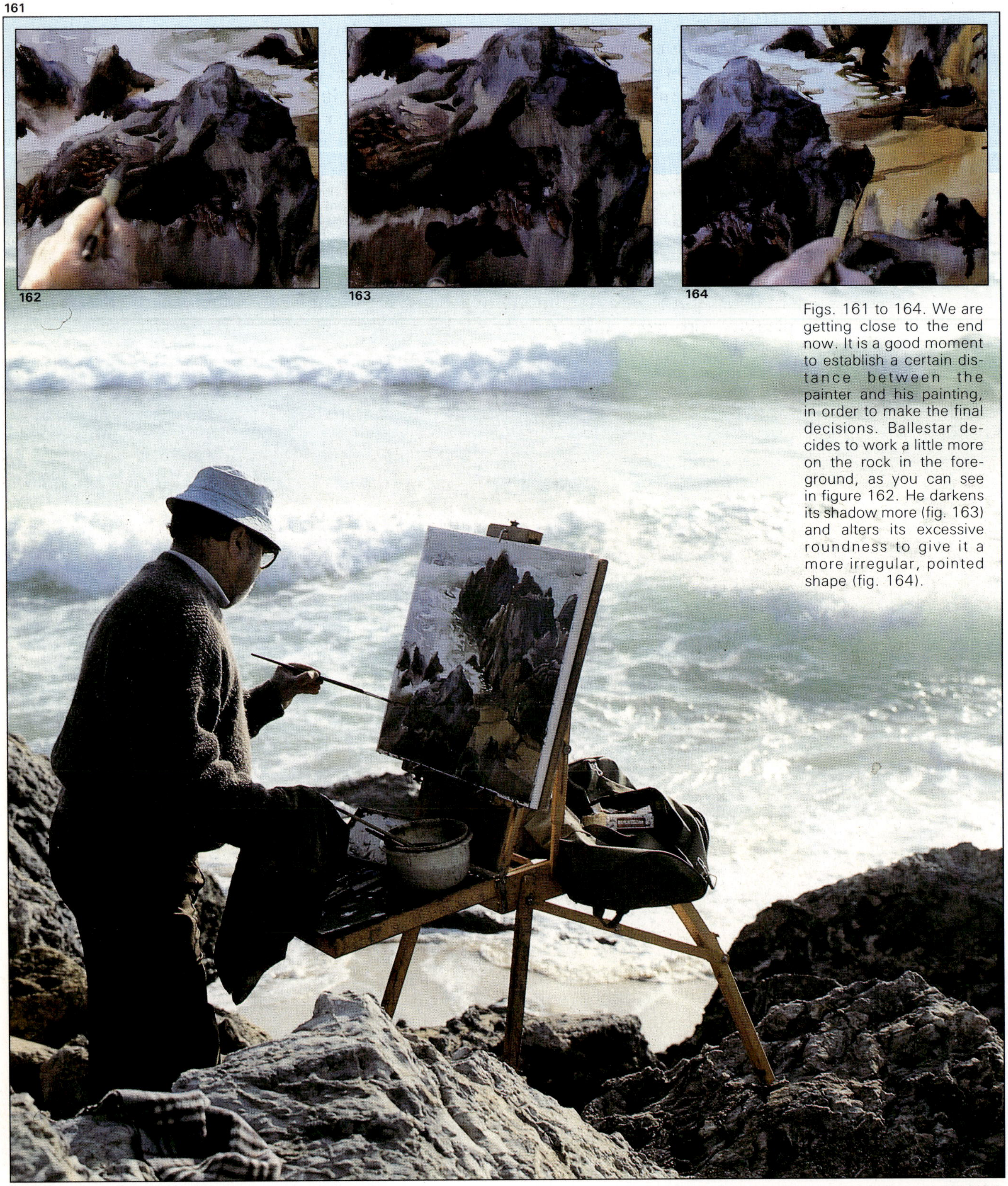

162

163

164

Figs. 161 to 164. We are getting close to the end now. It is a good moment to establish a certain distance between the painter and his painting, in order to make the final decisions. Ballestar decides to work a little more on the rock in the foreground, as you can see in figure 162. He darkens its shadow more (fig. 163) and alters its excessive roundness to give it a more irregular, pointed shape (fig. 164).

Fig. 165. From the start, Ballestar has made it clear that his intention was to make his central theme a pictorial one. To this end, he has chosen an apparently commonplace subject and managed to convert it into a fascinating exercise in color. The variety and richness of the tones he has used are striking, but do not in the slightest jeopardize the overall harmony of the watercolor.

Ballestar tells us that his work is coming to a conclusion. This is a good moment to take a short break from painting, step back a little, and take a look at his watercolor to decide what finishing touches are needed. To begin with, Ballestar finishes off the foreground. Preparing a fairly saturated violet-carmine on his palette, he spreads this mixture over the rock at the front of the picture. Though the color may seem rather dark now, it should be remembered that watercolors become noticeably paler once they dry. Suddenly, he notices an "unpleasant" roundness in the shape of the rock, making the pass between the two rock groups stand out too much. This is remedied simply by painting a small outcrop, which makes the shape less monotonous.

Ballestar's final brushstrokes are aimed at compensating any imbalances that may exist between the different tones and at various integrating zones, such as the rocks in the foreground on the right, which do not blend into the picture as a whole. Nevertheless, Ballestar feels that there are still a few small details which he will finish off in his studio.

165

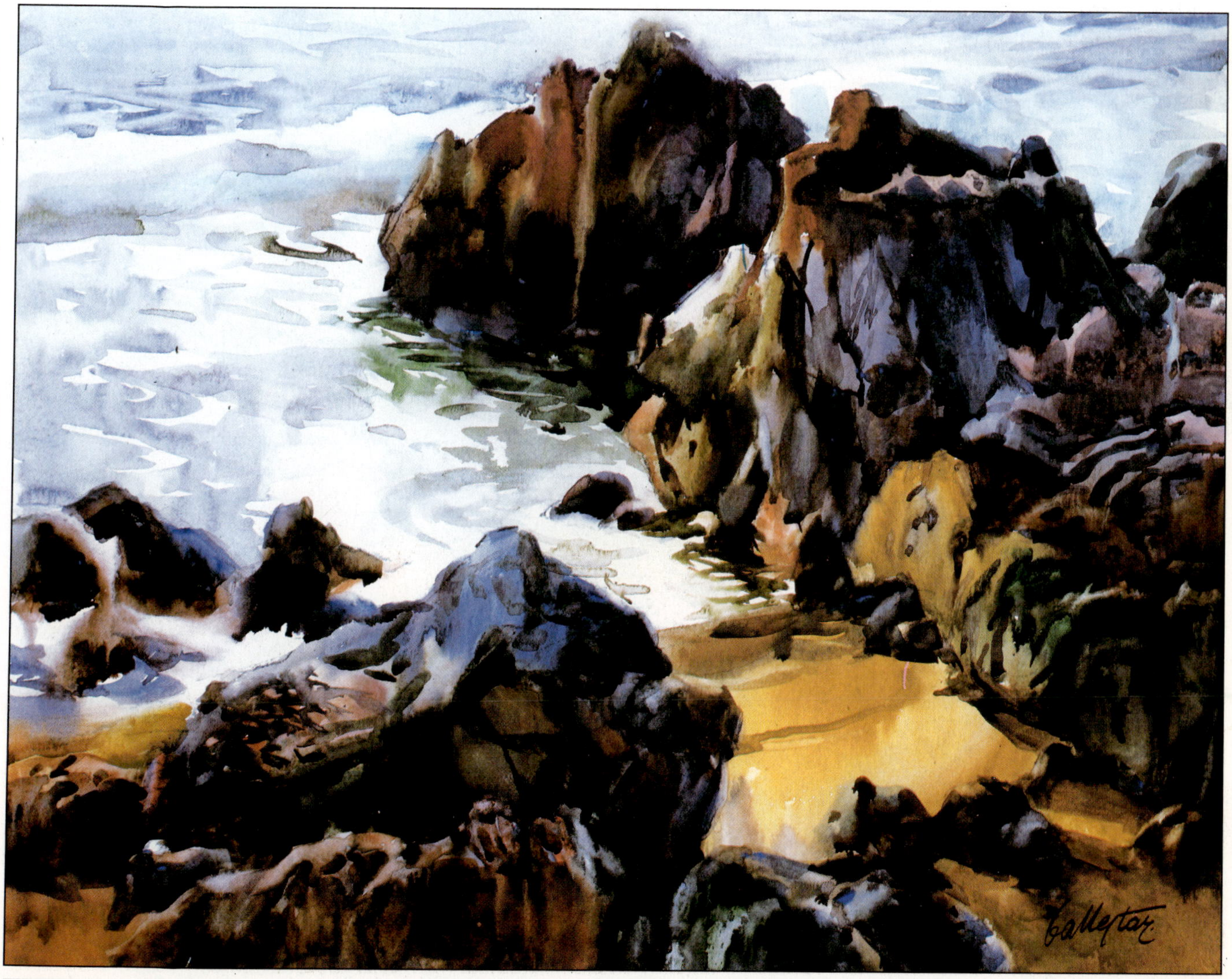

Contents